For Alex & Wanda Daffey

Good friends, &

Good colleagues in

joint ventures that

get no easier as

Remedial Law

time goes by.

But get more important

Many Thanks

Bob Wood

4/14/90

Remedial Law

When Courts Become
Administrators

**Edited by
Robert C. Wood**

**The University of
Massachusetts Press**
Amherst

Copyright © 1990 by
The University of Massachusetts Press
All rights reserved
Printed in the United States of America
LC 89-35720
ISBN 0-87023-698-9
Designed by Chris L. Hotvedt
Set in Sabon and Futura at Keystone Typesetting, Inc.
Printed and bound by Thomson-Shore

Library of Congress Cataloging-in-Publication Data
Remedial law : when courts become administrators / edited by Robert C.
    Wood.
        p. cm.
    Edited proceedings of a colloquium held Apr. 24–25, 1987 in honor of
Clement E. Vose, at Wesleyan University.
    Bibliography: p.
    ISBN 0–87023–698–9
    1. Judicial review of administrative acts—United States—Congresses.
2. Civil rights—United States—Congresses. I. Wood, Robert Coldwell,
1923–   . II. Vose, Clement E.
KF5425.A75R46   1990
347.73′12—dc20
[347.30712]   89–35720
                                                                CIP

British Library Cataloguing in Publication data are available.

This book is published with the support and cooperation of the University of
Massachusetts at Boston.

The perfect is ever the enemy of the good.

Old French proverb

Contents

Preface

This monograph is an account of a colloquium which took place at Wesleyan University on April 24–25, 1987, and focused on a relatively new but increasingly important aspect of American government—the continuing judicial intervention in the direct management and reform of executive departments and agencies. The prime justification judges and judicial scholars offer for court intrusion is the need to protect the constitutional rights of individuals over whom these public organizations have custody. This form of judicial activism is now known as *remedial law* and occurs when violations by public agencies of the rights of children, prisoners, patients, and tenants are found to exist.

Remedial law contrasts sharply with the cease and desist orders and awards of damages which courts issue when private parties have been offended. In place of these simple and straightforward measures, it entails deliberate, comprehensive, and often complex court efforts to change the organizational behavior of school systems, prisons, mental hospitals, and public housing authorities judged to violate individual rights.

The basic issue remedial law raises is how to reconcile the judicial value of equity with the organizational values of effectiveness and efficiency. Put another way, to what extent and under what conditions is judicial intervention likely to produce more effective public organizations better able to carry out their formal missions? For the colloquium, the specific charge was what reckoning can we make thirty years after *Brown* v. *Board of Education* introduced remedial law to American government?

The colloquium undertook this evaluation in honor of the late Clement E. Vose, the John E. Andrus Professor of Government at Wesleyan, whose distinguished scholarly career had largely been devoted to examining the interplay between American courts and interest groups. It brought together an eminent assembly of twenty-two practitioners and scholars—judges; court experts; school, prison, housing, and hospital administrators; lawyers active in key cases; and academic specialists in organizational theory and public policy. The participants were drawn from the courtrooms and institutions involved in four cases which represented the substantive areas of correction, education, mental health, and housing and illustrated each of the basic judicial oversight techniques—expert monitoring, courtroom review, receivership, and consent decree—which courts have come to employ to secure compliance with their orders. The scholars were authorities in the field, their credentials established by their publications and expert consultations in the field—hence, "wise owls" of organizational theory.

Histories of the four cases were written for the colloquium by Yale University graduate students in political science and management and provided to the participants in advance of the meeting to refresh memories of the participants who had been parties in the case and to provide the theorists with some stubborn facts. (The case histories are summarized in chapter 1 and presented in full in the appendixes.) The participants considered the cases in five intensive sessions, four of which consisted of presentations by the participants from the perspective of the court, the plaintiff, and the administrator. In the fifth session, the "wise owls" of organizational theory led the discussion.

Judge W. Arthur Garrity, who had presided over the Boston school desegregation case for more than a decade, began the deliberations with an overview of relevant law and its purpose and limitations. In a special evening meeting, the participants met in groups according to their particular roles—judges and experts, lawyers and administrators—to identify commonalities. A concluding session solicited views from observers invited from other colleges and universities. All proceedings were taped and transcribed.

What follows is the colloquium's collective judgment as recorded in the deliberations. The propositions and observations of the participants stand as delivered, arranged, recorded, and then reviewed by the participants according to the specific topics the colloquium had decided to address. For the most part, the participants speak for themselves, and then I have undertaken to synthesize, compare, and contrast their views. Occasionally I introduce propositions or document them by referring to the participants' own publications or to standard works in the field. But for the most part, the record speaks for itself, since the individuals the colloquium was fortunate enough to assemble constitute an extraordinary reservoir of experience and knowledge.

I am grateful to the Carnegie Corporation of New York and the Charles E. Culpeper and Henry R. Luce foundations for their generous support, to former president Colin Campbell of Wesleyan for his encouragement and participation, to my colleagues Russell D. Murphy who served as cochair for the colloquium, sociologist Charles C. Lemert, and Mary Ann S. Robbins, associate director of development, for their effective help. Special thanks go to Jane Tozer, conference coordinator, who oversaw travel and accommodation arrangements and provided the staff support which ensured a working environment so hospitable and attractive that work indeed was done.

Robert Wood
Middletown, Conn.
May 3, 1989

Remedial Law

One   *Framing the Issue*

A Conflict of Values

Can the constitutional rights of comparatively powerless people who are in the custody of public institutions be protected by courts without jeopardizing these institutions' major missions? Can public organizations be forced into strict observance of the Eighth and Fourteenth amendments to the United States Constitution?

These questions of public policy and public managment, and their ramifications, have been present and argued with increasing fervor for thirty years. They found their origins in the Supreme Court's landmark decision in *Brown I* and *II,* which authoritatively enjoined judges to prescribe plans by which public school systems would integrate children of different races in the same classrooms. Now the record of judicial intervention includes prisons, housing authorities, and hospitals for the mentally ill and retarded. For a generation at least, in almost every state in the nation, federal and state courts have isssued orders, promulgated standards, and prescribed administrative behavior designed to assure that the rights not only of schoolchildren but also of prisoners, patients, and residents in public housing projects are protected. An extraordinarily intricate web of judicial, legislative, and executive agency relationships has emerged to be reviewed, reaffirmed, modified, and occasionally set aside by higher courts. What responsible reckoning of these decades of court activity can be struck? Are the rights initially found to be violated by the custodial institutions now more secure? Have the institutions themselves been rendered better able to carry out their major missions? Can we develop models of court intervention that will increase the effectiveness of judicial intervention and reduce damage to the agencies involved? Finally, can court intervention be brought to cloture without losing the reforms so painfully generated?

Such was the charge to the Clement E. Vose Memorial Colloquium.

An Evaluation Process

Two stipulations governed the deliberations. First, the participants were asked to take as given the constitutional legitimacy of the doctrine of judicial activism that the record represents. We leave to legal debate the "true intentions" of the Founding Fathers and the propriety of the kind of judicial intervention that now is known as remedial law or institutional reform litigation. To be sure, along with Judge Arthur Garrity and Prof. Phillip Cooper, the other participants acknowledge that court personages and court doctrines change, and sometimes abruptly, over the years. As Judge Garrity observes, "Judges are not fungible. The judiciary has changed, and will change further. The big news is the fact that the current [Reagan] administration has appointed approximately half of the federal judges now sitting, and the watchword for selection in no mystery. The watchword is what is called 'judicial restraint.'" And Cooper identifies doctrinal changes during the Burger court, circa 1976. "We started seeing some dramatic changes by the court in terms of what it required to get a judgment at all, the availability of a remedy, its nature and scope and duration."

Nonetheless, changing judges, changing opinions acknowledged, the colloquium proceeded on the assumption that *remedial law in its essence of prescribing new patterns of organizational behavior is here to stay*—a twentieth-century component of American law, representing, in Don Horowitz's words, "a period of fundamental legal change, perhaps even comparable to the emergence of equity in fifteenth- to seventeenth-century England."

As a corollary, it was prepared to admit the bankruptcy of the executive and legislative branches in assuring the constitutional rights of the claimants and the woeful and willful neglect by the institutions involved. Courts intervened and remedial law was fashioned precisely because the other branches had abdicated responsibility.

The second stipulation was to take the judiciary at its collective word: *remedial law may go beyond the award of damages and cease and desist orders to mandate programs and administer changes, but it does not intend to "take over" public executive agencies permanently or manage them forever.* (Indeed, some participants, such as Judge Arthur Garrity, were skeptical that courts in fact intervened to manage at all—their foremost consideration on finding a constitutional violation and determining a liability was to find a remedy tailored to "cure" the offensive condition.) However broadly or narrowly court intervention is conceived or justified, at the same time all were to assume that the court in question would eventually "withdraw." So the Vose participants were enjoined to specify, if they could, the conditions which must prevail to allow a public organization to take charge of its own affairs once again.

With these stipulations, the participants were asked to focus their extensive collective wisdom on four cases brought in three federal courts and one state court. All participants, except the academic scholars, had been directly involved in one of the four cases. The cases were chosen to represent the principal arenas of remedial law: prisons, public schools, housing authorities, and facilities for persons with mental illness or mental retardation. They were also selected to represent the principal types of remedies devised in recent years: direct court oversight from the bench, assisted by experts or court-appointed monitors; consent decrees in which the plaintiffs and defendants came to apparent agreement; or, the most radical surgery, court-appointed receivers who assumed command of the agencies.

The Cases in Brief

Palmigiano v. *Garrahy* is a "prison" and a "monitor" case in Rhode Island characterized by continuing court involvement in which the role

---

[1]Full case studies of each case are found in the appendixes.

of lawyers in litigation procedures is substantial.[1] It was initiated amid a national tide of prisoner unrest and court-ordered reform in the early 1970s and continues down to the present time. After extensive hearings, temporary restraining orders, and repeated acts of violence, federal district judge Raymond Pettine issued a comprehensive order in 1977 directing massive changes in the state's correctional facilities.

Pettine's compliance mechanism was the appointment of a special master who made periodic reports and joined the court in detailed monitoring thereafter. Significant, though halting, improvement came in the late 1970s, but both the governor and the state legislature resisted the reforms, and the voters rejected prison bond issues in three referenda from 1978 to 1982. The sharp reduction in federal funds after 1981 and the dramatically increased inmate population led to the court's reentering the case with new orders in 1984, and it remained engaged at the time of the colloquium.

Keyes v. *School District No. 1* (Denver) is a "school" and a "monitor-expert" case and the first northern nonstatutory segregation case to come before the Supreme Court. The apparatus for implementation of court orders is more elaborate than in Rhode Island. Legally, *Keyes* is of special interest because of the Court's treatment of de facto as well as de jure segregation, the introduction of the "Hispanic" category as a class in education discrimination, and the widened scope of inference the Court allowed in holding that a localized area of internal segregation warranted a systemwide solution.

In policy and organizational terms, *Keyes* was originally hailed as a model of citizen participation and monitoring arrangements, featuring a Community Educational Council with several hundred trained citizen monitors and court-appointed experts to initiate and enforce a comprehensive desegregation plan. As the years went on, the effectiveness of these instruments in involving key elements of the community came under continued criticism, and the council was disbanded in 1984. The school district remains under Court order.

Perez v. *Boston Housing Authority*, a "housing" case, represents a further intervention of the judiciary into the public management process; indeed, it represents the most extreme strategy of involvement: *receivership*. It is a state case involving not the violation of federal or state constitutions but the Massachusetts sanitary code. Initiated in 1970 by public-housing tenants in Boston, with well-documented complaints on deplorable living conditions in the housing projects ("intolerable" in the court's judgment), the reform of the agency first was attempted through the monitor-master device, then by a consent decree. When both remedies failed, the court placed the agency in receivership in 1980.

In four years the receiver brought about a substantial restoration in the physical and social conditions of public housing in Boston, restructuring the management and control systems, securing major additional federal and state financial aid, improving security, and making some progress in collective bargaining agreements with the maintenance workers. In 1984 the court transferred authority to the mayor and eliminated the receivership. While a substantial restoration occurred, court oversight continues, and new allegations of discrimination and noncompliance have been filed.

Connecticut Association for Retarded Citizens v. *Thorne* is a federal and "constitutional rights" case, but it depicts a so-called happy ending through the consent decree mechanism, by which plaintiffs and defendants formally agree to a remedy for the violations asserted. Initiated in 1978 by a group of parents of mentally retarded children, and challenging the appropriateness and conditions of large, "in-house" long-term care facilities in the Mansfield Training Schools (in contrast to newer "deinstitutionalization" approaches), the case endured four years of bitter pretrial discovery, several months of negotiations, and six days of trial testimony before the state agreed to settle out of court. A month later, in May 1983, all parties except the labor unions involved agreed to a proposed consent decree which mandated four court monitors and the development of a comprehensive implementation plan.

Since then, although the pace of deinstitutionalization has been agonizingly slow, in the view of the parent group, new leadership in the department has begun a transition in attitude and operations. The consent decree remains in place, and the monitors, scheduled to leave in 1987, in their last report indicated "an atmosphere of lessening tension and increased cooperation."

Commonalities and Differences

As varied as these four sample cases are in many respects, they have two common features. First, they had been active for many years and were difficult to bring to cloture. The school litigation case (*Keyes* v. *School District No. 1*) lasted almost twenty years; the mental retardation case (*CARC* v. *Thorne*) lasted ten; the housing case (*Perez* v. *Boston Housing Authority*) lasted ten years from 1975 to 1984, when the authority of the receiver was vested in the mayor of Boston, who in 1987 remains under court order; the prison case (*Palmigiano* v. *Garrahy*) began in its present form in 1974 and in 1987 is still before the court.

The second commonality is that the litigation process produced findings of fact that overwhelmingly supported the plaintiffs' contentions that constitutional rights or statutory safeguards had been violated. A Denver school board intent on both segregating schools and denying equal resources to minority ones; a Rhode Island prison administration oblivious to the despicable conditions of its physical facilities and to the brutality and favoritism of its correctional officers; a Connecticut "training school" which allowed its patients to live in squalor; a Boston housing authority which consistently ignored ubiquitous violations of health and housing codes—all were guilty of flagrant neglect and harm to helpless people.

Beside these common elements, however, the cases diverge widely—in the style and temperament of the presiding judge, the ability and aggressiveness of the opposing counsels, and the attitudes and responsiveness of the accused administrators. The articulateness and cohesiveness of the plaintiffs vary widely from case to case. A judge dies, counsel for the defendant institutions come in and out through the revolving door of states' attorneys general, plaintiffs fight among themselves, administrators are fired or resign. Orders are issued, modified, withdrawn.

Nonetheless, sifting through the court findings and orders, legal briefs, and testimony produces some recurrent patterns of behavior and decision. What follows is the colloquium's collective "reckoning" of the impact of remedial law as it goes about reconciling the constitutional rights of plaintiffs with the execution of public program missions.

The next chapter acknowledges and describes the unsteady state of organization theory and discusses the issues involved in what we term site-specific organizations. Chapter 3 addresses several issues: the nature, terms, and limits of court intervention in public institutions; the power and limitations inherent in the judge's position and the ambiguity and limitations of judicial authority, particularly when a case lacks precedents; and the legal, political, social, and personal constraints involved, as well as the political and personal agendas that may influence a decision.

This chapter also compares and contrasts the legal mind-set and the administrative mind-set that commonly confront, confuse, and annoy each other in cases such as these; treats the uncertainties and complexities inherent in organizational reality and the environment; presents a five-stage process of remedial law; and discusses two special actors present in all remedial law cases—the experts and the lawyers—both of whom frequently have ill-defined roles and limited expertise in organizational behavior.

Chapter 4 raises the question of whether cooperation and partnership among the parties involved in the litigation process can flourish throughout the remedial process or whether the arena is destined to be adversarial. In particular, it considers the organizational responses to judicial intrusion, a range which includes resentment, ignoring or blocking efforts, minimal technical compliance, and, the most favorable and elusive, joining with the courts' efforts and embracing the opportunity to initiate reform.

Chapter 5 focuses on the larger environment of the organizations and actors which exist outside the formal boundaries of the courts and the organizations in question. These players both influence and are influenced by the central actors and are critical to facilitating or impeding the implementation of the remedy.

Chapter 6 considers the issue of organizational and judicial accountability. All parties agree that courts should disengage themselves as soon as possible from these cases, but the conditions under which complete withdrawal is recommended and the appropriate method of handling this disengagement is debatable. Minimalist and maximalist strategies appear, as well as those which lie somewhere in between, and a model remedial law process evolves.

This model brings together three key factors to be considered in initiating a remedy: the extent of the violations (broad or narrow); the capability of the target agency to institute and administer the remedy (high or low); and the disposition of the political culture (supportive or hostile). Through the use of this model, the colloquium proposes appropriate remedies, including direct oversight by the courts, consent decrees, and receivership. But first, we ask what we know in general about public organizations that have come under court oversight and their disposition to change in mission and behavior.

Two   *Changing Public Organizations*

The Unsteady State of Organizational Theory

It is best to be modest about the explanatory power of organizational theories—either classical or contemporary—and about their practical utility in solving specific problems that organizations face. No overarching single theory dominates the field today. As for prevailing theories, their capacity to provide persuasive understanding of how people behave in structured groups seems limited. More important, their operational usefulness—applying what we know about organizational behavior to specific situations such as institutional reform litigation—appears even more suspect. For most theorists at the Vose Colloquium, the factors that might explain how organizations come to be, how they work, or how they respond to interventions from the outside remain tantalizingly elusive.

Herbert Kaufman, the 1986 recipient of the John Gaus Award for distinguished scholarship in public administration, asserts bluntly that "organizational theory, at this stage of our knowledge, does not readily translate into operating handbooks of social change." Robert Katzmann observes that "organizational theory is very difficult to define and, unlike pornography, I'm not sure that we would know it when we saw it." He shares with Justice Oliver Wendell Holmes the conviction that "at times we have to chart our course by stars we cannot see." Shep Melnick remembers that the central lesson he took away from his first course in bureaucracy was, "It's a jungle out there." Alan Altshuler reminds us that as far back as 1946, Nobel laureate Herbert Simon characterized the study of public administration as essentially a laundry list of proverbs. "For most of the leading generalizations in the field of public administration, you could quote the generalization, and it sounded quite plausible—but there was another generalization that said precisely the opposite that was equally plausible." Although not as skeptical as his colleagues, Donald L. Horowitz holds that the operational rule of organizational theory is akin to Murphy's Law, "Be skeptical of what you're doing and how you go about it, because it isn't going to turn out quite as you think."

Skepticism about the power of organizational theory is accompanied by skepticism as to the unique nature of judicial intervention. Mark Moore, one of the observers invited to the colloquium, points out, "Organization theory tells us that organizations that survive over any period of time respond to the demands of their external environment." Kaufman pushes the point home—"Most theories of organization depict organizations as entities subject to a wide variety of environmental challenges. The impact of judicial intervention is just one more such challenge, and it is not different in kind from challenges by many other institutions—legislatures, elected executives, unions, professional associations, economic interests, and others. Organizational theorists may take note of the unique powers of the courts and of the unique constraints on them. But theories of organization can accommodate them without significant alteration."

As a point of departure, modesty about organizational theory and the special impact of judicial intervention is sensible. Our scholarship has progressed a considerable distance since the Weber and Taylor models of inflexible structure and rampant rationality were superseded by chiefly economic models which still assumed purpose, intentionality, and rationality. The Carnegie School especially has painted a different picture of decision making, characterizing institutions as "organized anarchies" and decision makers as possessing imperfect, limited information and beset by emotional and often unconscious factors shoving rationality aside.[1]

Making the distinction between public and private organizations is also useful. Harry Spence, the former court-appointed receiver for the Boston Housing Authority, confesses he misses "the mad humor" of public administration. "You get a wonderful sense about the craziness of this world and your obligation to keep moving. You have to be intensely political to solve the problems of an organization with a small p (the organic life of an organization) and a large P (the politics of the outside world)." John Moran, director of the Rhode Island Department of Corrections, dubbing himself "the garbage man," and James Scamman, appointed by the Denver School Board on a 4–3 vote ("They had eliminated all the other candidates and voted not to eliminate me"), confirm Spence's sense of a separate world. They agreed with the late Wallace Sayre, who found "the theory and practice of public and private management exactly alike in every unessential detail."

Focusing on public organizations alone, and using Kaufman's elemental definition of an organization as "the deliberate demarcation of boundaries that distinguish one set of people from all others, who take planned steps to admit, identify, and expel members and are structured as engines of activity that consume matter and energy," one finds agreement on at least one attribute of public organizations: extraordinary reluctance and resistance to change, especially when imposed from outside.[2] As Altshuler puts it, "Regulated parties squirm to get out from under regulations and constantly invent new forms of carrying on their traditional behavior." And Katzmann concurs: "We should always recognize the desire for autonomy of bureaucracies and the resistance to coordination among bureaucracies."

Kaufman identifies three internal reasons why organizations resist change, even when it is imperative for their continued existence in volatile environments. First, there are almost always contradictory

---

[1]The Carnegie School of decision making grew largely out of the work of Herbert Simon, James G. March, John P. Olsen, and Richard M. Cyert. The classic work on this is Herbert Simon, *Administrative Behavior* (New York: Macmillan, 1947).

[2]For the discussion here and in the next two paragraphs, see B. Shaw, "Knee Deep in the Big Muddy: A Study of Escalating Commitment to a Chosen Course of Action," 16 *Organizational Behavior and Human Performance* 27–44 (1976).

judgments by the organization's members as to whether change is necessary. Second, ineffective decision-making processes usually obtain. They tend to give more weight to personality (the glib, the loudest, the most fawning) than to analytical capability (the rational, the wise, the modest, the scrupulous). Finally, implementation of new directions is imperfect—slippage between decision and action occurs because the instructions are likely to be ambiguous or impractical or require that members cease what they are accustomed to doing and do something different.

Buttressing Kaufman's explanation of organizational resistance to change is the thesis of escalating commitment to the status quo—as identified, for example, by Shaw, who finds institutional officials, employees, and constituency groups emotionally, intellectually, financially, and structurally committed to an ongoing pattern of behavior and therefore "knee deep in the big muddy." This resistance to change is intensified when an individual or group perceives itself as personally responsible for an action or outcome, so that stubbornness compounds formal commitment and informal lethargy.

The defense of things as they are, deeply rooted in human anxiety about self-worth, the comfort of habit, and the fear of the new, was the initial consensus of practitioners and scholars alike as they considered the probable organizational impact of remedial law. Their assumption is buttressed by the mainstream of organizational literature from Robert Merton's classic analysis, "Bureaucratic Structure and Personality," through *Public Administration,* by Herbert Simon, Donald Smithbury, and Victor Thompson; *Inside Bureaucracy,* by Anthony Downs; to *Change in Organization,* by Paul Goodman et al. In short, whether their perspectives are "curative," as Arthur Garrity argues, or "reformative," as Paul Garrity took his public housing assignment to be, with remedial law the courts take on the toughest of organizational assignments—change. The cold comfort they are offered by contemporary organizational theories in going about this most difficult task is the proposition that organizational survival depends not so much on skill or flexibility as on sheer luck. Or as Kaufman counsels, "Since we simply do not have a good handle on causal relations in the field of organizational behavior, the soundest strategy for a society to adopt is to encourage a wide variety of putative adaptations to conditions that arouse significant discontent." Luck and experimentation, however, are slender reeds on which to rest the constitutional rights of nearly helpless people.

Site-Specific Organizations and Their Attributes

Not all the participants and observers at the Vose Colloquium accept Kaufman's dour view of the primitive state of organizational knowledge. Horowitz, for example, does not agree "that merely because we don't know everything in organizational theory we know practically nothing and that, therefore, we should scatter as many seeds as possible in the belief that the hardy ones will take root. We know very well that seeds produce weeds at least as readily as they produce flowers, and I don't think that we should abandon an attempt to understand what it is we are going to produce down the road."

Others point out that elite public organizations—those possessed with strong leadership, ample resources, a high degree of professionalism, and carefully structured tasks—are capable of timely and effective adaptation. They remind Kaufman that he recorded this capability in his classic study of the U.S. Forest Rangers and that management casebooks are filled with examples of more or less successful reorganizations of agencies and redefinitions of missions and altered behavior. Although the cynical motto of old Washington hands remains "Don't think, reorganize" (reflective of the instances when the appearance of change by juggling organization boxes covered business as usual for many federal bureaus), real change does occur in the adoption of new technology or when new problems with political saliency arise. The people who worked for Robert Moses and J. Edgar Hoover in their prime—the young Admiral Rickover, James Tobin of the New York Port Authority, Elmer Staats at GAO, Wilbur Cohen of HEW, all true public entrepreneurs—dramatically changed the behavior of their agencies, adjusted them to new conditions, and devised and implemented new programs with considerable success (Jameson W. Doig and Edwin C. Hargrove, *Leadership and Innovation* [Baltimore: The Johns Hopkins University Press, 1987]).

The problem with these examples of organizational change is not only that they are often highly visible national entities with important new missions but also that they are headquarters-field organizations. That is, their personnel work at stated times in stated places, and their clients usually come to their offices, do their business, and depart. Their behavior is governed by rules, regulations, and directives formulated at headquarters with the expectations of uniform responses in the field, which in fact frequently occur. Field-discretionary actions are routinely reviewed at headquarters, and often their performance is measurable in ways somewhat resembling the stereotypes of Weber, Taylor, Gulick, and Urlick—that is, highly structured by fashionable parables. They are not Michael Lipsky's "street level" bureaucracies: police, teachers, case workers endowed by the nature of their tasks with case-by-case discretion. Most important, they are not site-specific organizations where bureaucrats and clients coexist.

But it is site-specific organizations peopled by teachers, guards, physicians, nurses, hospital attendants, and building managers with which remedial law must usually deal. These organizations have visible physical structures in which "service-providers" and "service-receivers" live together continually or for a substantial portion of the day. There are aspects of communities here—entire cultures with mores and practices that are indigenous and with attitudes never described in manuals. They bear little resemblance to the offices of motor vehicle, employment, transportation, and economic development agencies. Nine to five is not the order of the day.

What goes on *inside* schools, prisons, housing projects, and hospitals is typically a mystery to public and elected officials alike until dramatic events occasion attention. Riots, sporadic legislative investigations, haphazard disclosure by media or public interest groups, legal motions, and petitions for intervention are necessary if the internal practices of site-specific organizations are to be revealed and observed. When they are uncovered, orthodox criteria of the formal distribution of authority within an agency, the degree of specialization of subunits, the professional status of personnel, relationships with other agencies and branches of government, and budgetary practices appear increasingly inapplicable. Site-based organizations simply do not work according to the usual rules.

Indeed when Alvin Bronstein was asked about the type of organization the Rhode Island Adult Correctional Institutions (ACI) represented (*Palmigiano* v. *Garraty*), he refused to answer. "On the organization of the agency, to answer questions about whether it was simple or complex, hierarchial or decentralized, is almost a waste of time. There was no organization. You couldn't categorize it. It didn't exist as an agency, as an organization. In terms of personnel, the union controlled job assignments. The union assigned the newest, least-experienced correctional officers to the most difficult slots because the older, wiser, more experienced people didn't want to work in the dangerous places. So you had the officers least capable of dealing with a particular situation being placed in the position of responsibility for those situations. That is not a way to run a prison."

As for leadership, Bronstein observes that "the agency's leadership at that time was strictly political in the worst sense of the word. The director of corrections was a friend/crony of the then governor. His background was that he had a degree in horticulture. At a court hearing I wanted to question him about the standards promulgated by the American Correctional Association [ACA], similar to the American Bar Association or American Medical Association for lawyers and doctors, and I said to him 'Are you familiar with the ACA standards in the 1977 edition?' And he said, 'What is the ACA?' "

As for professionalization, "The agency then, and today, has had a problem in recruiting and retaining personnel. Rhode Island is a small state, pay is not that good, and it is very difficult for them to recruit, particularly the kinds of personnel that are needed for the quasi-professional and professional jobs, like the dentists, nurses, and counselors. In those days there practically weren't any of them on board, and that's been a continuing problem all through the years. It's hard to believe that anyone in the government felt that the ACI was an efficient or effective organization with any degree of integrity. I can't say for a fact that I knew that the legislature and the governor realized that they were all a bunch of turkeys, but for them not to know would be a little bizarre."

John Moran, the director of the Rhode Island Department of Corrections, confirms Bronstein's observations concerning organizational incompetence and adds insights on the site-specific culture. Appointed in 1978, Moran insisted that he "run the place" and that there be no political interference. As former governor Licht said, who had interviewed him on an earlier occasion, "Mr. Moran, do you think that I'd want to put a friend to work in there?"

As to organization, when Moran arrived "the administration was paralyzed. They had locked the place up in August of 1977, and they didn't know how to get out of it. During that period, whatever might have been the relationship between the staff, principally the correctional officers, and the inmates was further exacerbated beyond belief because of the hatred that developed between the bars. People get very brave when people can't get at one another; there was tremendous hatred, tremendous hostility, people on the precipice of riot, people wanting to beat up if not kill others—virtually no aspect of the operation was functioning or acceptable by any kind of even minimal standard.

"We can talk about health care; we can talk about safety; we can talk about buildings and discipline, but the president of the union led the goon squad—a group of carefully selected weight lifters who, when there is trouble, do all the physical retaliation to inmates.

"When I got in there there was no structure, as Al said. There were all kinds of illegal activity, all kinds of favoritism. The most sophisticated prisoners, including some major organized-crime figures, had free rein of the institution, could do whatever they wanted to do, had illegal furloughs outside of the institution, had five-dollar cigars delivered to the front gate along with the lobster dinners when the ordinary inmate couldn't get a decent hamburger. The bottom line was that the majority of the staff was intimidated; they were afraid; they couldn't enforce the rules and regulations fairly and equitably.

"I became a one-man band. I didn't know who I could trust. I didn't know who was capable. I didn't know who was lying. I didn't know who the inmate leaders were, so I literally walked the cellblocks in the yard, probably eighteen hours a day for six months, so that I got to know the people. It was my hope from a management or organizational point of view to move forward and straighten the thing out with the people that were there. I made some drastic errors very early in the game in terms of the selection of personnel. I removed several people, principally the one directly responsible for the management of the maximum-security unit.

"There was the usual kind of conflict at that time, I am sorry to say, between the so-called treatment and program staff and the operational and uniformed personnel. I changed the structure. The uniform people were under one assistant director. The treatment staff—the educators, psychologists, counselors, chaplains, whatever—were under another assistant director. It was like a United Nations kind of thing. Problems would develop down on one level, but they could never be resolved. By the time they filtered through three or four different levels, they never were resolved. They were lost in the shuffle. Legitimate grievances, from inmates and staff alike, were never addressed.

"So I changed the structure. I eliminated one division. We began to attack what I call the basics, to call things as they happen, to hide nothing, to make it known to all, staff and inmates alike, that we were not going to run this thing on the basis of fear, with billy clubs. Very early in the game (and it's not unimportant to the essence of this colloquium), we had to show to the inmates, as well as the staff, that the staff as well as the inmates would be held accountable for illegal activities. A major situation developed again when the goon squad beat up an inmate.

"Now we get into a larger political kind of governmental arena in that I pressed for a grand jury indictment on that. I would tell you that we did not succeed. The best we got out of it was a short-term voluntary demotion of a few lower-level staff people. As an aside, we had a dentist there—you won't believe this one—who was so intimidated that he extracted eyeteeth unnecessarily to give to a particular inmate power broker who in turn made necklaces out of them and sold them.

"As for on-site culture, contrary to what you might hear, there is no such thing as a prison country club. It is an entirely different world, an entirely different culture, an entirely different set of norms with its own formal organizations, philosophies, conflicts. It deals with an entirely different kind of client population—if you will, a citizen population—namely, the inmates themselves. The prison world is very complex. No matter what the abilities or the philosophies or the commitment of the managers or administrators may be on any level, it's a jungle. Deaths can occur, robberies occur, rapes occur; there's brutality between inmates, toward staff, staff to inmates. So it is a different setting.

"When I arrived in February 1978, we had about 600 inmates, with 140 of these in protective custody. Protective custody means that for one reason or another they cannot live safely in the prison population. Again, as part of the horror of the prison culture, there's a kind of caste system there. You know, 'I'm fine, I'm all-American, I'm normal, I'm decent if I'm an armed robber. But if I'm a child molester, or rapist, or whatever, I'm in trouble.' The percentage of the people we have in that category depends upon the fairness—and the ability and the consistency—of the management of the place to protect them. They were not being protected.

"As a last resort I transferred out the twelve inmate leaders who had a stranglehold on the institution. Nine o'clock at night they were gone. We had to bring them back (and I tell you this only to indicate the degree of the total collapse of the operation) for formal classification hearings, and people had to come in, and this was a full, formal trial before the federal court. The inmates were represented by a premier criminal attorney in the state. Everybody thought they were good boys but me, our staff had been so intimidated.

"These were the people that had a stranglehold on the institution and that were at the root of much of the violence, rape, and so on that was going on. We were so intimidated that we couldn't even get people to go in and recite their criminal record. But we won that trial, and they went off. A few are dead now, but since then, all the rest have been brought back but one."

Not just in prisons, however, are primitive organizational structures superimposed on special cultures. *CARC* v. *Thorne* is a case in which parents of mentally retarded persons brought suit to require the Connecticut Department of Mental Retardation to pursue the policy option of deinstitutionalization—placing patients in community residences and halfway houses as an alternative to keeping them in large institutions such as Mansfield Training School. In the mid-seventies Mansfield had a population exceeding one thousand, and Connecticut had the second-highest rate of institutionalization in the country. Gary Thorne, then the commissioner for mental retardation, was viewed by the parents as giving lip service to community services but being professionally committed to the preservation and upgrading of the large institutions under his authority. In the view of the present commissioner, Brian Lensink, the site-specific mental retardation institutions "had been built on a very dictatorial and authoritarian approach to management, very internally directed. The average stay of a manager was something like twenty-five years. They were very much entrenched in the direction that they had been going, even though the previous commissioner had left."

David Shaw, counsel for the plaintiffs, describes the conditions circa 1978. "I'll never forget our expert tours through the school's hospital. Thirty or forty profoundly retarded, nonambulatory people were in diapers, lying on the floor on a hundred-degree day, with the windows open, bug killers up on the wall (they were having no effect). Staff were attempting to feed these people with flies running all over them, dirty diapers piled up in the corner. The smell of feces and urine was sickening. During that period of time, one-third of the institutional population at any one time would be injured each month, including about 10 percent of that group, which would sustain what were called serious injuries, severe laceration, or death.

"The conditions were worse for the most disabled. The programs were the worst. The conditions were the worst. The state did not support severely handicapped people in the community. And as a result, by default, they wound up in the state institution. There were no services for them at the state institution either, and since there was no place in the community developed to support their needs, they remained in the institution forever. The average length of stay during this period of time was some twenty-five years.

"The studies done during this time showed that the lack of programming was overwhelming. For example, of the four hundred people who needed some toilet-training program, virtually none of them received it. Of the three hundred people who needed some assistance in walking or ambulation, virtually none had such training. And it goes on and on and on—dressing, feeding, basic things like communication, trying to communicate your needs to someone else—no program."

With deinstitutionalization under way by the court-initiated consent decree, Commissioner Lensink is now undertaking to manage a different and more demanding organizational change. To him, knowledge of organizational change and how an organization works is essential. "You must know both the organizational structure you are leaving (the institutional model) and the community organizational structure, the model that you are trying to develop. They are very different animals, and it's like managing two totally different industries—heavy iron works and modern technology—you can't compare the two, they're so different. This is what often makes the organizational change difficult. You are trying to evolve a system that has run institutions into one that can now run community programs, and that is not an overnight process. This evolution or revolution takes a rather dramatic change in perception and organization."

Much the same organizational maladaptation and depressed culture pertained to the Boston Housing Authority (BHA). Former state superior court judge Paul Garrity characterizes the circumstances he discovered in presiding over *Perez* v. *Boston Housing Authority,* where the violations were not of constitutional rights but of explicit provisions of the state sanitary code. As to managerial competence, "One of the five commissioners of the housing authority, a person who had been appointed to that position by a former mayor of the city of Boston, who was the designated treasurer of the agency, did not know that if there was a column of figures, a line, and under that line a parenthesis between the numbers on the bottom with a minus sign in front of that parenthesis that that indicated a deficit.

"The board was also somewhat corrupt. People in the developments were desperately in need of refrigerators, and the tenant representative to the board had two in her office. She had one for her beer and one for her baloney sandwiches, or whatever she kept in those refrigerators. Again, people in the projects had had work orders filed on their behalf seeking a refrigerator for six or seven months. They didn't have any place to keep their food in their units. The difficulty with respect to maintenance was the union contracts, which said it took five people to fix a toilet bowl."

Court-appointed expert Robert Whittlesey's monitoring reports documented organizational deficiencies more formally. "During the 1960s, BHA went through several major administrative changes, but none of these resulted in an authority capable of coping with the worsening physical state of its developments or of adapting itself to a changing clientele. The current problems at BHA are a legacy of the inability of prior BHA boards and staffs to resolve growing difficulties in public housing management. In August 1967, a coalition of public interest organizations in Boston concluded, among other findings, that:

—Hiring policies at the BHA remain essentially 'closed.' Most housing authority positions are regarded as being in the patronage category, to be filled by directive from city hall.

—The 'life tenure' system for housing authority employees, enacted in 1962, has led to severe personnel problems at the BHA. The system leads to poor work performance and inadequate supervisory mechanisms.

—Many of Boston's housing projects (particularly those for the nonelderly) are in need of major and minor repairs, and in some instances wholesale remodeling. The quality of maintenance in most projects is far below acceptable standards.

"The five-member board of commissioners hired and fired all staff, awarded all contracts, and sometimes arranged for private firms to work for BHA without contracts. Board members personally selected the tenants for many BHA developments."

As for housing conditions, Whittlesey's statistical documentation of a 19 percent vacancy rate and code violations so extensive that $50 million would be required to bring the sixteen thousand apartments into conformance, is vividly portrayed by one of Garrity's visits to a project. "I can recall one fairly poignant instance, touring one of the more distressed developments, where the roof had been installed improperly because the BHA had inadequately supervised its installation. And after a day or so of rain, the water would soak into the building, and maybe about a week later, when it was sunny outside, as I found out to my distress when I went into a first-floor apartment, it was like a tropical rain forest. Literally globs of water were coming into this particular apartment where there were youngsters running around the floor with umbrellas and rubber boots on, and they had to stay there because they had no place else to live. And that wasn't the worst. I'm sure many of you have seen *Apocalypse Now,* which depicted the fall of Saigon. Some of the conditions in many of the developments resembled what was depicted in that film: dumpsters were on fire, dope dealing was going on, people were being mugged, people were screaming from the buildings, 'I haven't had electricity for two or three weeks'— absolutely horrific and terribly bizarre."

Even schools, a mixed version of headquarters-field and site-specific organizations, bear similarities to their around-the-clock institutional colleagues. As Willis Hawley, a court-appointed monitor for the *Keyes* case, points out, "Schools have been described as loosely coupled systems, and that is particularly true here. And those of you who are organization theory experts may want to engage Chester Barnard's notion that the membership of a school is not just the bureaucracy and the people who work in it, but it's the kids and the parents. And if you think about the mechanisms for control that a school system has over all those parts, you can see that they diminish significantly as you move away from the board, the superintendent, then the staff, and all the way down; as is true in any organization, those linkages become attenuated. But when you get to parents, they become virtually nonexistent. And of course, you can't control or move them, the obvious choices that a parent has. But the ways of involving parents and engaging them are often difficult to do."

After hearing John Moran's account of life in Rhode Island prisons, school superintendent James Scamman expresses a sense of comradeship. "I can't believe the comparability of two positions given the whole difference in field. John and I are both immersed in the here and now—keep it happening, keep the doors open—and my usual mind-set is, 'Are we going to survive until 4:30' (or in my case, 10:30 at night each day) and then get up and assault the barricades once more at six o'clock the next morning?"

He continues, "No one on the board, no one in central staff, except myself and a couple of others, have ever engaged in planning. They never engaged in an organizational plan for a school system. They don't know how to deal with the simplistics of census-tract data, student and enrollment projections. We have a huge computer and have spent millions of dollars on one of the most expensive student data bases in the country. But we've never used it to produce any reports or structure any files. But there are little guys with moss behind their ears and green eyeshades and yellow pencils who have dedicated their lives for twenty years to trying to build a good solid information base. Which we don't use!"

Historically, school cultures were relatively stable: student bodies were made homogeneous by neighborhood housing patterns; teachers were predominantly women; and the organizations were "flat," with only the hierarchy of principals, assistant principals, and coaches. Families were outwardly united, with their children's education regarded as a special value. Changing society and desegregation introduced a new climate of turbulence which John Finger, first court expert for the Denver School, captures.

"The process of desegregating the schools created such extensive upheaval that many schools, students, parents, and teachers were pushed to the limits of their tolerance and capability. Black students suffered. Their schools were closed. They endured most of the busing. They were bused to the suburbs under metropolitan plans. They were transferred from school to school, for many were disenfranchised and had no neighborhood school or regular school to which they were assigned. Some black students, having attended the worst of the segregated schools in both the North and South, schools far worse than most of us ever imagined or cared to admit existed, were suddenly thrust into desegregated schools, and schools where middle-class values predominated. Different value systems clashed. Turfs and rights were disputed. Desired racial harmony and understandings became hostility and hate. Teachers suffered. Some found themselves unable to adapt to the educational needs and differing values in desegregated schools. Segregated schools were not completely eliminated. An underclass, composed mainly of the black minority, persisted."

Inauspicious Circumstances

Ronald Melzer, a monitor in the Connecticut case, observes that the challenge which the reform of site-specific organizations poses for judicial intervention in the name of constitutional rights reminds him of a card he once got from his wife. The cover announced, "Happy anniversary, dear. You are the answer to all my dreams." On the inside it said, "You're not exactly what I dreamed for, but you're obviously the answer."

If the organizational theorists in the Vose Colloquium, while differing as to the operational utility of present-day organizational theory, agree that comprehensive change is the most difficult assignment for public managers to undertake, the testimony of the practitioners makes clear that the organizations the courts addressed are the most unlikely candidates for reform. As a nationally famous civil rights lawyer, who invented the legal doctrine of attacking the "totality of prison conditions," Al Bronstein could assert in the Rhode Island case that, "put simplistically, the defendants, the state officials, have the power to cure the disease of unconstitutional conditions. They might not like to do it. They may not want to do it, but they have within their hands the power to do it. It is all so doable. The question is, will they ever do it?"

But his optimism that where there is the will, a way comes easily, finds few supporters among his colleagues. As participant after participant describes the simple awfulness of the institutional conditions that prevailed, the carefully constructed search for proximate cause which

Arthur Garrity followed to identify "cures" for unconstitutional conditions in the Boston schools pales before the pervasiveness of the failures of the institutions involved, the "totality" of violations. Bronstein comments, "In this "prison pie," each segment represents a different piece: overcrowding, classification, medical care, food, idleness."

The awesomeness of the failures is, of course, compounded by the incompetence of the organizations: patronage ridden in some cases, unprofessional in behavior, unsophisticated in organization structure and task definition, sometimes corrupt. Even the schools, closest perhaps to professional in aspirations, have been so long wrapped in the cocoon of their special governance structures, separated from other governments and programs, proclaiming their unique function, maintaining their flat organizations, that when intervention came, they were singularly ill equipped to respond: naive, inexperienced in the ways of other organizations, and most particularly, unfamiliar with adult, political confrontation.

In short, although amply justified in taking action by the clear and flagrant constitutional violations, the courts perforce grasp the stickiest thistle imaginable, prescribing the most arduous organizational endeavor—widespread, wrenching change—on the least competent organizations. They assign to the "softest" organizations the "hardest" assignments—injunctions to change their ways, to shift their behavior, and, most difficult of all, to respond to these injunctions imposed from the outside.

It is little wonder that the colloquium's explorations yielded so few easy answers and recorded no instance of unmitigated success. As an instrument for simultaneously securing individual rights and the achievement of program mission, remedial law was certainly not what courts "had dreamed of." It was, however, at least an answer. How effective an answer remains to be considered.

Three   *The Nature and Limits of Court Intervention*

The Grand Illusion

The popular stereotype of remedial law intervention, powerfully buttressed by the media, is of the undisputed, overarching preeminence of judicial authority. John Finger, the expert in *Keyes,* witnessed such an assertion of superior power while seated in the federal courtroom in Denver. He was there to help his friends in the NAACP Legal Defense Fund who were representing the plaintiffs, and he recalls, "I almost didn't go to court that day. I had planned to go home, but I decided to stay over another day and watch the court proceedings. And I'm sitting there in court and all of a sudden Judge Doyle announced that I am his consultant. So I moved from the table with my friends in the defense fund and went to sit with his law clerks."

Thereafter, as Finger mapped the demography of the school district and worked to develop a desegregation plan, he learned Judge Doyle's basic modus operandi: "My job is to decide. Sometimes I'm right. Sometimes I'm wrong. If I'm wrong the boys up there [the circuit court of appeals] will tell me so."

"So if I said to him, 'You have to desegregate Cheltanham; you can't leave an all-Hispanic school,' Judge Doyle's response was, 'Those parents over there just got a brand new school with all that new equipment in it; I'm not going to let you move those children out of that school.' And when I said to him, 'Part-time pairing won't work; and anyway, the courts will overturn you,' his response was, 'It's my business to decide what to do, not yours. I'll take care of the law. You make the part-time pairing work. What do you think I hired you for anyway?'

"He was concerned about the school department's initial reluctance to assist me. 'Are they giving you all the help you need? If they won't help you, you just let me know. I can take care of them.'

"The *one* key player is the court, and if the court says he's going to have part-time pairing, that's what he's going to have. And if the court says, 'I'm not going to close that school,' that's the way it's going to be.

"I tried to close the Ebert School, and the judge said, 'What are you closing that for?' My response was, 'It's no good; it's a little tiny school. I don't want it.' And the court said, 'They just want to sell that school. They told you to close that school because they can sell the land that that school is on. That's worth a lot of money. And don't let them close Morey because that sits on a very expensive piece of property. And they want to sell it so they can build our new administration building. Don't you let them do that.' "

Perceived power—as many a political science textbook asserts—is real power, even if it is blue smoke and mirrors. To Finger, although the subsequent years demonstrated that the consultant's plan was not self-executing, Judge Doyle perceived himself in charge. But Judge Doyle knew the limits of his power. "After he decided on the desegregation plan and had appointed Denver's Community Monitoring Commission, he sent me over to talk to them. 'Tell them I've done my job. It's not up to me to implement the plan nor to sell desegregation to the community. You go tell them that I've chosen them because they are the community's leaders. What happens now is up to them.' " And years later, Superintendent Scamman testifies to the persuasive, continuing impact of the court, as he tried to establish his own executive authority.

"One phenomenon is what I would call the 'blame the judge/judge as protector' phenomenon. Whether or not those of you from the legal world would agree, the existence of the supervision or the maintenance of jurisdiction over an institution is enormously powerful psychologically. Whether or not the judge has direct power to do a lot of things, I don't know, but as a psychological phenomenon, that power is enormous. It cannot be underestimated. It affects almost every aspect of everything that goes on in the whole organization, whether inside or outside the bureaucracy. Politically the whole sort of psyche or ethos of the community is affected by that phenomenon. Just the fact that it is there changes the thinking about everybody.

"Take the role of school principals, for example. They'd use the judge as an excuse for everything. If they did something that the parents didn't like, they would say, 'The court requires we do it.' Then the parents would acquiesce. On the other hand, if they didn't want to do it, they'd say, 'We can't do it because of the court, because of the judge.' So, the mystical powers of the overlord of the whole operation and the psychology of the systems permeated the whole thing.

"The teachers' union acted the same way. If the union wanted to do something to cooperate with us, the court 'allowed' it; if it didn't like our proposal, its lawyers would say, 'The court says no.' And that is a whole big mind-set that is far more insidious even than perhaps I've indicated. On the flip side, of course, is this whole notion that the existence of the court order, the role of the judge, is to protect the rights of those who have needed, and still need, access to the community, so as long as he's here, everything is fine."

In law and in fact, of course, judges are not free agents. Not only are they subject to the strictures of judicial proceedings, the adversarial model of adjudication, and review by higher courts, but a host of other constraints appear. Phillip Cooper puts it this way. "The judge is caught up in the law of political interface because he or she is called upon to perform a kind of unique task—that is to say, to reconcile demands for rule-of-law concerns, on the one hand, with pragmatic understanding of the political environment in the year he or she operates, on the other. We've had different views, starting with Judge Garrity, who talked about the notion of curative but not reformative purpose, and the limitation of remedial orders to specific violations, very much the rule-of-law approach, to a discussion by some practitioners yesterday who said, 'Look, here are the realities; here's what works; that's what we have to do.'

"The problem of the judge is to ignore neither. The judge cannot ignore either one of those and have any kind of successful outcome. The fact is, that despite the wide-ranging discussion of what's possible for courts to do, we've seen a lot of remedial decree judgments, liability judgments, and remedies overturned on appeal. One reason for that is, precisely, the failure to deal with the rule-of-law concerns adequately within a situation in which everybody recognizes the need to be pragmatic about what's going on around the court.

"Two kinds of limitations therefore arise. First, doctrinal limitations: What it required to get a judgment at all, the availability of a remedy, etc. Second, judicial policy range considerations: What the court can do, pragmatically, apart from the question of precedence and rule-of-law limitations. Here the correct questions are, 'What were the problems presented to the court? What options were accorded to the court? What constraints were placed upon the court?' I would say the judge cannot be a free agent, a rational actor who has unlimited range of choice and all options available to policy-making. Constraints imposed by other actors in the executive branch, by federal litigation strategy, and by the capacity of the participants to present the case effectively can literally make the judge a captive—of lawyers, organizations, and organizational actors themselves, who are not free agents outside the process."

The Legal Mind-Set

If Cooper effectively disposes of the judge as a free agent or *the* single actor, nonetheless, Finger demonstrates that he or she will be a central figure. Crucial to understanding the effectiveness of intervention in securing change is an appreciation of the legal mind, so often at odds with those of both administrators and social scientists. Don Horowitz focuses on this phenomenon, citing the Thomas Reed Powell maxim: "If you can think about something that is intimately related to something else without thinking about the thing to which it is related, then you have what is called a legal mind."

Horowitz is concerned with the appropriateness of the adjudicative process to the issue of institutional reform, confessing an "uneasy sense that static thinking is going on in a dynamic environment. Controversies that do not involve disputes between individual litigants, but rather disputes over broad policies or over the way in which public institutions are to be run, are clothed in the raiment of complaint and answer, discovery, trial, and decree. The garments are ill fitting, but they are worn. By and large the cases are handled as if they involve disputes between individual parties—which is why the revelation that they really do not has come as something of a shock. For this, there are no doubt many reasons: the attractiveness (for all the participants) of casting something new in the garb of something established, disagreement about just what alternative mode might be apt for these cases, and—perhaps above all—the predictable response that such a proposal regarding a public agency and not an individual would indicate that the issues are not appropriate for the courts. For, at bottom, the adjudicative mode—particularly, the resolution according to law of controversies between individual litigants—lies at the core of what courts do and are expected to do. Even when they do something different, it is usually cast in the adjudicative mold."

To Horowitz, the legal mode of reasoning, which is deliberately controversial, skewed by stare decisis, and narrowed by the rules of evidence, is ill equipped to deal with the subtle issues inherent in site-specific organizations. The law has difficulty accepting the proposition that gray is the color of truth. Finally, since its central feature is *finality*—rendering conclusive judgment—the adjucative process is often clumsy in adjusting to new circumstances.

Even more important, the process has difficulty in understanding the managerial mind. Harry Spence, the receiver for the Boston Housing Authority, notes, "The problem always, if you're an administrator in that process dealing with court systems, is that the very manner of thinking which a court brings to the problem that allows it to be the intervener, to break the logjam, is also deeply disabling to then solving the problem. The rational insistence that words have meaning, that those words shall be held to their meaning, and that power is to be ignored in asserting that those words have meaning, absolutely disempowers you for bureaucratic solutions. The moment that I become a receiver I have to be intensely political to solve the problems of an organization, and the reasons are not ones I can state in court because the court can't take cognizance of the categories I have to think in.

"So there are two sets or categories of thinking—legal and managerial—and they have to do with the function of words and whether words are to clarify or to obfuscate and whether they are to resolve problems or to clarify problems. And the way in which people think and the categories under which the court thinks have to be so different from the categories in which the political process moves."

Robert Wood experienced the collision of the two mind-sets directly when, as superintendent of the Boston Public Schools, he presented the court with two simultaneous equations proving that, given the white flight from the schools, he no longer had a sufficient number of white students to meet the racial composition ratios for individual schools established by court order three years earlier. "That's a matter for Dr. Einstein," the court declared; "under our rules, it's not evidence."

The Uncertain Process

If the judge is not all-powerful in shaping remedial law and if the legal mode of reasoning is at odds with managerial thinking, then the process of litigation by which violations are found and remedies ordered becomes critical. Law scholars such as Abram Chayes applaud the very "fuzziness" in which the process of public law litigation seems typically to work, where only a tenuous link between rights and remedies is initially established and rights really evolve in subsequent negotiation, trial and error, experimentation—somewhat in the spirit of the work of Prof. Herbert Kaufman. Most Vose participants, however, are less enthusiastic, tending to agree with Horowitz that the garments of complaint and answer, discovery, trial, and decree are "ill fitting."

Phillip Cooper presents the most comprehensive model of the legal process in five stages: the "triggering" event, the finding of liability, the fashioning of remedy, the postdecree phase (when "a foreign body"—monitor, master, or receiver—intrudes upon the organization), and remedy refinement.[1] His substantial research indicates that the overwhelming majority of remedial law cases arise from some unanticipated and unplanned event: a riot, a personnel layoff, a tenant frustrated to the point of rage, an aggressive or public-spirited lawyer who reads of a wrong in the local newspaper and seeks to right it. The triggering event may provoke a reaction to historic policies and practices, may bring national forces into play, but it is essentially unpredictable.

Once the event "triggers," however, and voluntary access to the court is sought, the plot thickens. "At the time of triggering, all past

---

[1]Phillip J. Cooper, *Hard Judicial Choices: Federal Court Orders and State and Local Officials* (New York: Oxford University Press, 1987).

events come together, and the case is not about one issue, but a series of potential issues that have been lying out there waiting for a trigger. So most prison cases don't present one issue. They have one issue that triggers them, whether it's double-celling, change in medical conditions, or whatever, but once triggered, any given issue area brings out the other panoply of issues waiting in the wings for organizations that have to confront them. And the judge has that problem."

The litigation phase compounds the judge's problem. Here, in Cooper's view, the issue is capacity. "Not just the judge's capacity, the court's capacity, but the capacity of the participants to present the case effectively. The judge is, in some sense, a captive of the lawyers who argue the case, and of the agencies who present it. The organizational relationship is in part affected by those people set up as the communicators between organizations and the court, placing dramatic limits on what the court can do."

The skill of the attorneys in establishing an adequate record—their knowledge of case law, their ability to locate and work with expert witnesses, their case management if other parties are involved—all affect the options available for remedy. So do the skills of defendant counsel. Al Bronstein, one of the nation's most illustrious plaintiff counsels, comments on the quality of his legal adversaries in the Rhode Island prison case. "The quite senior assistant attorney general who defended the state of Rhode Island had a level of competence which was probably somewhat greater than my one-and-a-half-year-old grandchild, but certainly not as competent as my three-and-a-half-year-old son. He was then promoted to be counsel to the governor, but he was a total bungler who had no understanding of what the case was about and no understanding of federal rules of evidence. Since then, in the last eight years, there have been about twelve different assistant attorney generals who have represented the defendants in this case. Their tenure lasts anywhere from three to eighteen months, each one comes in not knowing the history of the case, what was said in chambers or in status conferences, which are often not transcribed.

"So I have a special responsibility: I have to teach all of the defense lawyers what the case is about. They were all relatively inexperienced, particularly in federal court and in constitutional law. They tend to be quite young, some more intelligent than others. And I think the state has been badly served by the level of competence. And that, it seems to me makes a difference in dragging out the litigation and complicating it unnecessarily. And that's been my experience over the last twenty-five years of civil rights litigation in a variety of areas where the state or a state agency has been the defendant: they are badly served by generally less than competent counsel." Moreover, the judges' disposition to show "due deference" to executive agencies, to reduce conflict, to understate the gravity of the offense, as Cooper shows, may further skew the litigation.

By the time the phase of remedy-crafting arrives, the judge's options are shaped powerfully by what has transpired in the litigation phase. Cooper notes further, "The role options available to a judge may be dictated by the parties to a case. If the parties are willing to negotiate, the judge can be a facilitator. If the parties refuse to negotiate, the judge becomes, in effect, a ratifier. In general, the remedies are not developed out of whole cloth by the judge but are presented by the plaintiffs. It then becomes the problem of the judge to determine what portions of the proposed remedy the court will order and enforce. That's a somewhat different notion than the question, 'What should the judge do?' as though the judge were an independent actor merely sitting down at the desk and deciding what the outcome should be. In many if not in most cases, remedies are driven by the parties, even if the judge doesn't ultimately agree to what they want.

"Indeed, the judge is sometimes called upon to play a court defender role, defending the court against efforts to use it as leverage in a case where the court's leverage position can bring problems for the court. Indeed, at one point during the *Wyatt* v. *Stickney* case—the landmark case in mental health litigation—during the hearings, Judge Johnson exclaimed in open court, 'I will not have this court used to get a budget out of the legislature of the State of Alabama.'

"The court is also concerned about its own capacity to do its other business. The court has to arrange its relationship with the other organizations so as to protect its own core technology, its ability to handle the several hundred other cases pending on the docket. So, in part, role option is not a free-agent question but in part an interactive question. What can the judge choose? That's in part limited by what the parties permit."

Other participants believe that the remedial phase shows the judiciary at its weakest. Horowitz observes, "Courts know a good bit more about declaring rights than they do about framing remedies, so they need to devote more time to puzzling through what might achieve the court's objectives. Courts are impatient with this phase of the case. They want to settle things once and for all, even though they have come to learn at this point that the case is going to bounce back from time to time."

Shep Melnick doubts that many remedies "operationalize" goals and rights with sufficient clarity; they fail to "spell them out." Robert Katzmann agrees: "For most judges the difficulty is that, by training, their concern is not with how organizations operate. Many of them have their formative experience in private law firms. Most of them don't have experience with the management of bureaucracies." Or as Marshall Kaplan observes at this key juncture of the interface between law and politics, "Judges are poor politicians and probably poor anthropologists. Managerially they lack legitimate operational definitions of output measures. They are unable to predict second-order consequences or to secure sustained organizational role changes."

Alan Altshuler sums up, "Judges are prisoners of their expectations, the traditions of their set of institutions, and are often fundamentally at odds with the political system. The courts in the sense of desegregation cases have articulated some constitutional principles which have to do with a guilt determination—positive acts of discrimination which almost lock the door against judicial intervention to deal with the social facts of the case."

To the legal mind, the problem may be seen as sheer failure of will or malevolent intent on the part of the agency. In his August 1977 decision in *Palmigiano* v. *Garrahy,* Judge Raymond Pettine wrote,

> The experts were unanimously agreed, and the court finds, that there is a complete absence of effective leadership or management capability on the part of the responsible officials. The problems catalogued herein are not new. They have been highlighted by a succession of advisory commissions and paid consultants engaged by the governor or the department to untangle the reasons for the collapse of an effective, orderly, humanely habitable prison in Rhode Island. The findings of each of these studies admitted into evidence have been reconfirmed and underscored by the evidence presented at trial.

Yet, speaking of the succeeding decade, Bronstein reports that "on at least a dozen occasions over the last ten years, I have been in either the courtroom or in chambers when problems were presented to the judge, and the judge takes off his glasses and glances at me. 'What can I do? What shall I do? Tell me Brother Bronstein' (that's what he calls me when he gets angry). 'Tell me Brother Bronstein, what shall I do? How can I make this thing change?' That's the level of frustration. Putting it simplistically, the defendants—the state officials—have the power to cure the disease of constitutional violations."

To Bronstein, the issue is a moral one. "The defendants *can* do these things. Until state officials do everything that they have the power to do, they cannot complain about court intervention, because in classic equity terms, they've come into court with dirty hands."

This sense of moral indignation produced remedial strategies and arrangements which many of the Vose participants found to be excessively simplistic. From his five years of research, Cooper identifies three "core" remedy options: *process remedies,* involving such parainstitutional arrangements as advisory committees, citizen participation requirements, and educational programs; *performance standards,* mandating specified school enrollment ratios, personnel, facilities, staffing levels, numbers and types of rehabilitated housing units, and diagnostic schedules; and *specified particular actions,* including school busing or required changes in hospital rooms or prison cells, which are spelled out in the decree. Most remedies, as in the cases on which the colloquium focused, are a composite of these options advanced either simultaneously or sequentially as the courts found unsatisfactory progress toward redressing the violations.

As to the implementation techniques to effect the remedies, three approaches have also emerged, reflecting the degree to which a judge is disposed to "trust" a target agency or display due deference to the executive. The court may *directly oversee compliance* from the bench, either by requiring periodic reports from the agency or through the use of monitors and masters who serve as intelligence agents. Here, the organizations are left largely on their own as to the means to achieve the goals. Alternatively, the parties involved can *enter into a consent decree*—a mutually agreed to, formally specified, and legally binding plan or process—which the judge approves and which assumes continuing cooperation among the parties. Here, administrative discretion is much more limited, as the Connecticut case demonstrates, because the plaintiffs or monitors are a continuing presence and coequal parties in the negotiations. Finally, the court may take over, its patience exhausted by the evident ineffectiveness of direct oversight or consent-decree negotiations in securing compliance, and *place the agency in receivership,* substituting its administration for the previous one. This was the final step in the Boston housing case, after the eighteen-month effort of a master to effect a consent decree proved ineffective. In Paul Garrity's words, "At that point there was no choice but to take over the authority and to appoint my own person to run it."

What concerns the Vose participants in examining both the options and instruments in crafting remedies are the limits to organizational feasibility. Cooper notes that administrators as defendants rarely, if ever, signal the courts what they believe it is possible to do. "The judge cannot know what the consequences and problems will be in implementation unless there is an argument on such matters as political, administrative, fiscal, and technical feasibility. Yet in the cases that I've studied over the last five years, in no case did the unit of government involved present, on the record, a formal case in the remedy process as to why on fiscal and administrative terms it could not perform the remedy called for. There was a great deal of generalized discussion, but in no case was there a formal argument as to capacity and ability. In the remedy-crafting process the judge is in part constrained by what administrators are willing and able to do themselves in directing the performance of the court."

Horowitz details the consequences of overlooking the "heterogeneity" within target institutions. "We've already had our attention called to union contracts. Of course, the union contract won't override the judicial decree, but it may skew the implementation of that decree in a big way because the administrator will feel bound, insofar as it's within his power to agree, to abide by the protections of the contract. And that may skew the nature of the remedy that the administrator feels able to provide.

"Are some pieces of the solution altogether outside the control of the defendant organization? Almost certainly they will be—the personnel managers, for example, in the Connecticut retardation cases, or for that matter, the state judges who sentence more people to prison as federal judges declare war on overcrowding. Another obvious constraint is budgetary resources. Those, of course, are usually outside the defendant's control."

Horowitz goes on to describe the failure of remedial orders to anticipate second- and third-order consequences. "If a court authoritatively declares that it wants X units of Y, most defendants can, at some cost, provide X units of Y in order to comply. But the cost is often an intrusion into other values the court would protect if it knew what the cost would be. In a school case, if you want a certain pupil-teacher ratio, you can have it—but only by skewing the distribution of special subject teachers, who are not the kind the court thought it was moving around in the system.

"Why is this? Because regular classroom teachers may have some greater protection against transfer than special subject teachers. So if you want a certain pupil-teacher ratio, or a certain expenditure per pupil, you may have it. You can get it year after year, but you may have a surfeit of art teachers at one school and no art teachers at another school.

"Do you want to mainstream the retarded? Fine. But the next case may involve the retarded homeless. To put it differently, what you get depends on exactly what you ask for, which then affects what constraints impinge on the defendant organization and what resources will be available to it and what strategies the organization will resort to in order to achieve compliance. This, needless to say, argues for asking carefully what to ask for, if you are the judge, and it argues for being nimble about changing the request, as nimble as the defendants are about complying in ways that the court hadn't anticipated."

If the trigger phase is unpredictable, the litigation phase heavily dependent on the skills of the participants, and the remedial phase often failing to address organizational issues, it is little wonder that affairs often do not go well in Cooper's postdecree and remedy-refinement phases. Except in those few instances when the judge goes it alone directly from the bench, a "foreign body" is usually implanted in the organization in the form of expert, master, monitoring body, or receiver. The issue is whether the host organ receives or rejects the implant.

Sometimes, as Denver school superintendent James Scamman observes, "some of us find it so comfortable working for judges rather than our normal bosses that we may not actually want to be out from court order." More frequently, the presence of a court-appointed master seems to irritate and offend. Conceding the constitutional justification for Judge Pettine's entering the Rhode Island decision, acknowledging the undefensible conditions that then prevailed, John Moran listed the accomplishments in the state's prison building program ($50 million and two new institutions), a sixfold increase in the adult services program, and the addition of hundreds of new staff. Yet, the master is still present as Moran undertakes to determine the site for a new medium-security institution, and increasingly Moran believes "we are dealing now with minutiae like everyday scheduling, which had better be left to people that understand priorities and understand our corrections." And Scamman complains that as the postremedial phase runs on, accompanied by feedback, refinement, and amendment, he experiences the phenomenon of "moving goalposts." "My guess is that if John Elway had led the long drive against the Cleveland Browns but he didn't know whether the goal posts were 80 yards, 90 yards, or 110 yards down the field, he probably would not have been successful in mounting the drive which actually won the championship.

"There's a concern that if the case is terminated too early, the objectives won't be achieved, that we must come up with new standards and new issues. And that has really been discouraging to the board and to the central staff when they think they have about got a handle on the whole problem and all of a sudden a new issue comes up.

"And I don't at all criticize the judge for that. I think it is a phenomenon of the plaintiffs' trying desperately to find areas in which we haven't yet complied and which we need more work in order to keep jurisdiction going. And so, we have given up entirely trying to negotiate a solution or working positively with the plaintiffs because every time we do what they ask, they come up with something else. And the judge has recognized that, but it has been a frustration in terms of trying—my objective was to try to negotiate a settlement so that all parties were happy and we didn't have to have a final decision by the judge, that it could actually be a convergence of all the interested parties. I've given that up because I don't think the plaintiffs are capable of doing that. They think that continued jurisdiction is necessary, and they'll try to do almost anything to maintain that.

"Judge Maitch indicated in his June 3 opinion that his concern was for the constitutional rights of students yet unborn. And I've wrestled with that day and night for the last eighteen months, understanding what he means, but trying to wrestle with how, in good conscience, as a person that has to advocate for the freedom of the institution to manage itself, I can help build in some of those protections, to answer that question and still not sacrifice the integrity of the institution for decades to come."

Even possessed with the substantial powers of receivership, Harry Spence concurs. "You can't wait until everything is cured, because there isn't a single apartment building in the city of Boston that doesn't have some code violations in it. If you said we've got to get rid of every single code violation before the court can be out, you know you are in there forever. You are attempting to get to a state that is impossible."

At the heart of the problem in the postdecree and refinement phases is what Cooper and Elaine Johansen identify as *conflict conversion,* referring to the work of Nathan Caplan in utilization theory. As Johansen summarizes, "Utilization theory suggest a process of ownership and reinvention of information and policy by the organization affected. Utilization is greatly influenced by the function the information or policy serves to organizational interest." Conversion occurs by a process of "rejection and reincorporation of ideas, or reinvention where ideas are 'sanitized' before they are incorporated into practice, transformed so that innovation is invented on the inside, not implemented from the outside."

For Johansen, "The conversion process comes about by careful and diplomatic negotiations," and signs of it are apparent in the consent-decree process of the Connecticut case. Yet, as the Connecticut participants acknowledged, "The transformation is a delicate undertaking."

David Shaw defines the basic objective of the consent degree. "The primary emphasis of the decree was on setting up a quality assurance system that would look at the individual class members on a periodic basis to determine whether they were improving, whether they were regressing, whether they were truly integrated with society; it would measure their progress so all of us involved in the case could determine whether we were succeeding in our role in the case or not. Significantly as well, the consent decree required the state to identify what we knew to be very significant barriers to providing decent programs and community placements for class members. I mentioned the Medicaid rates and the rates of group homes. But we were very concerned about identifying barriers to lasting change and to addressing those barriers."

And Ronald Melzer speaks of the monitoring skills involved. "One of the things that was very clear to us was that we had no interest in being police because that was not a particularly creative thing to do and, after all, anyone could develop checklists and see how well things were doing. Nor did we have any desire to run a second system, because we already had a system of our own, which I think gave us a different perspective on our role—one that might have been different, let's say, from someone who'd never had an opportunity to run a service system and would look at being a monitor as an opportunity to do just that.

"All of us had a tremendous desire to teach. And at least the plaintiffs very early on made it clear to us that they wanted us to teach and that they really wanted us to help to design a new system in Connecticut. We all knew enough about other consent decrees to know that the creation of a privileged class can have very poor effects on the development of entire service systems. So we had a great desire to make sure that whatever we did, and in whichever way we helped, we would always try to suggest ways of doing business that would, in fact, make sense for an entire service system.

"Now, it's one thing to have great desire, but that doesn't go very far without opportunity. No one envisioned that the consent decree would necessarily create opportunity in the way that it did. But the fact is that shortly after the signing of the consent decree the administration changed, and we had, for approximately one year, an interim administration, which for the most part knew nothing about the field of mental retardation. And we suggested, humbly, that maybe it would make sense after years and years of fighting if all the parties could come together again, and rather than having an implementation plan that was designed simply by the Department of Mental Retardation and handed down, wouldn't it be nice if all the participants—which included service providers, advocates, the union, and the parents' association—could get together and perhaps design an implementation plan together. And, in fact, that's exactly what happened. I really need to underscore the importance of serendipity here because, had we not had that change in administration, I honestly believe that all the motivation would not necessarily have produced the outcomes that we had."

Opportunity, serendipity, a disposition to teach, monitors who were already running other mental retardation systems and did not want to take on another—these seem very special circumstances in Connecticut in a case in which the consent decree (as of 1987) is not yet three years old. At rock bottom, Johansen's and Cooper's postulate that conflict conversion is essential in the postremedy stage suggests that the capabilities and dispositions of the actors involved have to be of the highest order and that their tasks are perhaps the most demanding of all. The question naturally arises—and was largely unexplored in the colloquium—as to how the parties came together, with what motives and expectations they fashioned their agreements, how they selected the monitors if such were employed, and how they determined progress to be satisfactory.

Writing elsewhere and in reviewing other cases, Cooper provides a cautionary warning concerning the troublesome nature of consent-decree administration, despite the apparent savings of time and costs in avoiding protracted litigation. "Discerning plaintiffs may be wary of the consent decree because of the risk of finding themselves in a false negotiation. A negotiated agreement may be false by intent or by circumstance. The fact that one sits down at a table is no guarantee of an intention to play the kind of non-zero-sum game that will lead to settlement. Second, one may bargain at the margins but not expect to produce a strong remedy on the core issues. Most decrees contain some form of waiver provision or escape clause which can be exploited to one degree or another. A third form of false bargain is the repudiated negotiation. The players change and later governors or agency heads may not consider agreements made by their predecessors acceptable. Similarly, there is no assurance of compliance even if the executive branch does intend to conduct legitimate negotiations and expects to implement the agreement. State legislators rarely consider themselves bound by such a process. Finally, if there are difficulties encountered later in implementation, there is less of a record in a negotiation than in a formal proceeding to support further action."[2]

Melnick concurs: "Administrators who accept consent decrees are signing pacts with the devil. Consent decrees can help them get more money from state legislatures and overcome some personnel restrictions. The price they pay is significant: they allow the plaintiffs to look over their shoulder and to question their authority. This can demoralize the entire organization."

[2]Ibid.

Two Special Actors

If the five-phase process of remedial law litigation emerges as fraught with uncertainty and unexpected barriers, there are two actors in the process whose roles seem to be consistently strong and consistently negative in impact. They are the experts and the lawyers, both for the plaintiff and, as Bronstein earlier made abundantly clear, the defendants.

About experts, Vose participants emphasize two characteristics. The first is that their expertise is typically in the substantive field of the case, such as education, mental retardation, penology, or housing. They typically are not—and they do not pretend to be—professionally conversant with organizational behavior or the political behavior of the relevant culture in which the case is embedded. The second is that their role is frequently ill defined and appears almost mysterious, often secretive, so much so that their activities rarely become part of the formal record. If they carry their own professional agenda, they can transform the work of the court. Melnick observes that "many of the institutions involved in litigation had for years tolerated horrid conditions that 'shock the conscience.' But the response of the courts has not been to define which of these conditions are horrible and how they must be changed. Rather, they have asked 'experts' how these institutions should be run. These 'experts' have an agenda much more extensive than merely correcting gross abuses.

"Cases involving care for the retarded provide a graphic illustration of this. Judges took on these cases because the retarded were living in buildings which were at times frigid and at other times stifling hot; because they received little medical care and inadequate diet; because they were restrained for long periods of time and physically abused. Before long, however, judges were embracing fashionable ideas about deinstitutionalization. They were claiming that all retarded citizens have a right to 'develop their full potential.' When the Supreme Court decided the *Youngberg* case—which said, in effect, that the constitutional rights of the retarded are limited to the provision of safe and healthy care—most legal commentators and advocates for the retarded claimed that the Burger court was showing itself to be reactionary once again. My reaction to the case was that the Court did a very good job defining the constitutional problem and staking out a job which judges could actually perform."

Reporting on the informal discussion among court-appointed experts at the colloquium, Judge Arthur Garrity, who presided over the Boston desegregation case, emphasizes the expert's "novel, unique role covering a multitude of functions" and the extent to which the special relationship of the expert to the court constrains full and free negotiations with all parties that the consent decree appears to require. "Generally speaking the function of the expert depends on a particular problem confronting the court at the time. It's sort of a crisis management role, and the authority of the expert oftentimes changes—it expands or contracts during the course of the litigation. And there are fewer scholarly articles written on the role and responsibilities of court-appointed masters and agents than perhaps any other branch of the topic."

Mort Tenzer of the University of Connecticut is more direct. "Because most experts are subject-matter experts, judges might think of inviting people who are experts on administration to help in choosing remedies which are sensitive to organizational matters, for example, explicit consideration of administrative procedures and administrative theory. James Scamman concurs: "Expert witnesses ought to be people who are experts in organizational change as well as some of the other phenomena."

Reflecting on his experience in Denver, as one of three expert members of the Compliance Assistance Panel, "brought in on the theory that if enough information was pumped into the system, rational people would make the right decisions," Willis Hawley reports, "Our panel has no authority, and it begins to whine a little bit, like a puppy. Some of the letters that we wrote to the board in retrospect sound pathetic, 'Come on, you guys, please.' Because what's happening, of course, is presumably neutral. We are very aware of that. We were all people who were known as advocates of civil rights, and we are trying very hard not to be the directive; at the same time, you find yourself pushed into an adversarial position in these matters. I don't think there are any neutrals in this game."

Experts, however qualified, tend to grate on the nerves of administrators, as Moran and Scamman make clear throughout the proceedings. Duke University's Don Horowitz observes that "expert testimony helps inform the judge's view of what's wrong and what the correct posture of the subject organization ought to be. But, of course, to be qualified to testify as an expert you have to have some credentials, usually paper credentials, in a particular field of expertise—often, in these cases, the social sciences. What this sometimes means is that academic experts have the advantage in court at the expense of practitioners. It also means that what courts end up doing is adjudicating one theory of treatment at the expense of another. Or to put it a little more sharply and provocatively, the courts are implicitly and occasionally explicitly, in such cases, declaring scientific truth as well as legal norms. Scientific truth in the social sciences, needless to say, is often ephemeral. These declarations are frequently accompanied by a change of organizational leadership, as we have witnessed in this colloquium quite graphically. And often the new leadership of the organization adheres to the newer theories sanctioned by the experts. And we saw the perfect closing of this circle when in Connecticut the plaintiffs' expert became the defendant."

If the participants sometimes view the experts as loose cannons and argue that their role and recruitment should be more carefully attended, they are even more scathing in their judgment about the deleterious behavior of many lawyers in the cases—lawyers too often without real or effective clients. Robert Whittlesey speaks on the Boston housing case: "The housing authority hired outside litigators to defend them, and I don't think they ever understood their role. That legal firm made our life very difficult, and, for instance, the negotiations of the consent decree, starting from a general consensus about what you ought to do, took eleven months to put in place. And Judge [Paul] Garrity had over two hundred hours where we'd sit and hammer out word by word, and the tactic of the law firm was to impinge as much as it could, the right of the court to move. And therefore, my role in this consent decree got more and more confined, and more and more dead-end roads were put in there to defend the authority in that sense.

"There was a kind of corrosive effect of the litigating attorneys against any sort of cooperative arrangement of working with the authority. For example, the consent decree gave me a role in the employment of all the personnel in the authority. I knew when we signed that consent decree that the administrator wanted to leave and the opportunity would come up for a new administrator. As soon as that administrator announced that he was going to leave, the lawyers took the position that that position was not personnel of the authority and would fight the court on our right to be party to that appointment. That battle was central to what we were doing. I think of all things that had happened in the term of that consent decree, it was the obvious fight by the lawyers (supported by the board which thought the lawyers were really doing the best thing for them) that was a totally corrosive thing."

John Finger describes his first meeting with the Denver school superintendent. "When I went to see him, he sat down at a glass-topped table, and right in front of me was Snoopy—'Happiness is a neighborhood school.' And not only that, he's got his lawyer with him, and he is not going to talk to me without his lawyer. Well, we sashay around about that a while, and I finally think the best thing to do is to say, 'Fine, I'll see you tomorrow. I want to come back and talk to some of your school staff.' I didn't want to say what I was going to say in front of a lawyer, and I didn't want to get in trouble because here I was a brand new consultant to the judge."

Later on, Willis Hawley finds a similar condition. "The attorney named by the school board is Michael Jackson. For some period of months the school board, through Jackson, professed their commitment to the process that the judge had set up. At the same time, however, nothing ever came back from the board. The Compliance Assistance Panel worked very hard to avoid giving direction, at the same time giving direction. We first started out with broad guidelines. We then started with more specific guidelines, then tried schedules. But the attorney stifled response. We came to call him 'Stonewall' Jackson."

Today, still in Denver, James Scamman feels the same way about Don Horowitz's "free-floating lawyers." "Regarding attorneys, the whole attorney-client relationship needs to be disciplined differently for both plaintiffs and defendants alike. These kinds of litigations cannot become lifetime occupations for attorneys. There are enormous fees involved and enormously complex cases, and in many cases it becomes an incentive for not settling and not getting the resolution brought about for either the plaintiffs or the defendants. In fact, the attorneys themselves sometimes become obstacles to the process. The plaintiffs have a reason to keep the case in court and keep moving goalposts and bringing up new issues. In fact, the defendants themselves, who may be involved in some political kinds of things, may be not working toward positive solutions either. So it is not to point fingers necessarily at either side." John Moran was even more direct:

"Prison litigation has become an industry. It is an industry in and of itself. A lot of people make a living off of it."

In effect, at least twenty years of experience with remedal law at both federal and state levels has yielded no clear, most-favored general strategy for curative remedies. Some broad regularities in the litigation process are identifiable, and the constructive performance of at least two of the actors in the cases can be called into question. One thing is certain: the judges' decisions are not bolts from the blue or unrestrained commands from on high, as the media frequently depict them. On the contrary they are the product of a host of variables, beginning with the possibly accidental trigger and the personalities of the judge and the other participants and ranging through protracted phases of litigation. Kaufman's "chance and circumstance" seem indeed to play a major role in the tediously constructed remedies and implementation. As with all human enterprises, whimsy and accident are present.

And this is but a part of the story. Matching the strategy and tactics of what is clearly a limited judicial role are the strategies and tactics of the bureaucracies affected. This dimension consumed an equivalent amount of the Vose participants' attention.

Four   *The Quicksand of Bureaucracy*

In his 1985 *Public Administration Review* article "The Politics of Partnership," Shep Melnick traces the evolution since 1971 of what Judge David Bazelon of the circuit court of appeals called "a new era in the long and fruitful collaboration of administrative agencies and reviewing courts—[a] judicial administrative partnership." Consisting principally of new requirements in the rule-making provisions of the Administrative Procedures Act, the courts called for "open, fair, and rational decision making," including public disclosure of administrative records, participation by all affected interests, a heavier reliance on legislative history in interpreting statutory objectives, and more extensive application of the private right of action. In Melnick's view, so pivotal has the courts' role become that he is tempted to speak of the "iron rectangle" in policy-making in place of the traditional "iron triangle" political scientists have long identified—legislative subcommittee, agency, and interest group. Yet what the courts call "partnership" and "collaboration," Melnick points out, administrators view as "a clever disguise for judicial usurpation of administrative authority." Resentful of being criticized for acting arbitrarily, parochially, and sloppily, department and agency heads increasingly ask, "With partners like this, who needs enemies?"

In remedial cases, where constitutional rights were clearly violated, the "partnership" assumes an interaction of special intensity, since far more than the application of new rules and procedures is involved. One way or another direct participation in managerial decision making occurs, and in Alan Altshuler's words, "administrators squirm and wiggle" to adjust to the new circumstances. As Paul Samuelson once wrote regarding the theory of public choice, "One man's circus is another man's poison," and for many an administrator working under court orders, the presence of masters and experts, the constraints of a consent decree, and the specter of possible receivership appear poisonous indeed.

The Client Enthroned

Perhaps the most galling feature of institutional reform litigation, at least as perceived by the administrators, is that the very people they perceive themselves to be helping suddenly appear as hostile plaintiffs, angrily challenging the administrators' professional credibility. To be sure, in the cases of schools and mental institutions articulate parents and families from the outside are usually the catalysts for action, not the inmates or tenants from within the institutions who, in Elaine Johansen's words, "recognize that they are not only dispossessed but despised." Yet, even in schools and mental health cases, administrators are inclined to feel that plaintiffs are biting the hands that feed them.

Margaret Dignoti describes the origins of the Connecticut Association for Retarded Children (CARC) and the perceived reactions to it of the commissioner for mental retardation, Gary Thorne. "We were formed by local associations that spontaneously, and unknown to one another, developed around the year 1950 in our society across the country. It's a social phenomenon that's never really been explained. Why parents in the 1949 to 1951 years in our society banded together and said, 'We will no longer accept the fact that we have to keep our kids home,' or as the phrase was then known, 'in the closet until such time as we can put them on the waiting lists for the big institutions,' which were all that were in existence then. The parents, mostly women

49

in those days (I think the forerunner of the feminists of today, very gutsy and very courageous women), banded together, began to have bake sales. And they prevailed upon local ministers and rabbis to give them space in church halls, etc. And they hired teachers, many of them teachers that were staying home in those days to raise their own families, to get the kids together that had mental retardation and start teaching them so they could prove to society at large that these kids could indeed learn, because as parents they knew that and they had to prove that. And they did. And they did it beautifully.

"In the 1950s their aim primarily was to get the public schools to allow their kids to be educated, and to obtain a free and appropriate education. And CARC sponsored a number of bills during the 1950s, and by 1959 was successful in achieving the first mandatory special education law in the country. In the 1960s we went to the legislature and focused on the adult population that we didn't want to have go to another institution that was then in the planning stage—at the time, the waiting list for Mansfield and Southbury training schools was sizable and growing. We convinced the legislature to divide the state into twelve regions and develop a regional office or a small institution in each of the regions, thus bringing the services closer to the families and helping the families to maintain their children at home. Hopefully, then, we could develop small-group homes and facilities in the community. That was working very well in Connecticut by the late 1960s.

"In the early 1970s a couple of unfortunate things happened simultaneously that reversed our prior success. A new commissioner was hired by the name of Gary Thorne who gave lip service to the belief in community services but who at heart believed that many people with mental retardation should live in institutions. And at the same time Congress passed a piece of legislation under the Title XIX Act that assisted the states. It was an institutionally biased piece of legislation written with a good heart, but in effect this piece of legislation said to the states, if you will bring your pretty awful institutions up to federal physical plant standards and programming standards, we will reimburse you a portion of the cost of operating those institutions.

"The commissioner went after the almighty federal dollar with a vengeance. He asked us to put on hold our dreams and our visions for our loved ones with mental retardation until all his institutions were up-to-scale and the federal money would be pouring in. And then he would go about and reinstitute the development of the community services we so desperately wanted and had fought for. We rejected that, and during the 1970s we battled the commissioner and the legislature in every session, and we lost badly just about every time. It was kind of a David vs. Goliath situation, with us attempting to educate the commissioner. He kept telling the legislature that we as parents and advocates really weren't as experienced as he was. After all, he had had thirty-three years in the field of mental retardation—to which we sometimes snidely replied behind his back, 'One year of experience repeated thirty-two times.' And every time we made an inch forward in changing public attitudes, our commissioner would go on public television, or some other media forum, and would make comments to the effect that our bill in the legislature to force the state to allow people in institutions to wear their own clothes was a ridiculous bill because retarded people had a tendency to eat their clothes.

"We didn't know much as parents and advocates about constitutional law. But we knew enough to know that the Constitution protected people in the sense that they can't be deprived of their liberty and they should be free from harm. And we knew these people were being locked up and they were being harmed. And with that we turned to the attorneys, and we said to them, 'Please help us.' "

Mort Tenzer would challenge Dignoti's characterization of Commissioner Thorne and her claim of effectiveness for the clients and their representatives in achieving reform. "I really take issue as a professional in the field. To say that you believe in something puts you into the realm of affirming apple pie. Performance is what most of the litigations haven't required and what I think is really the criterion. Commissioner Thorne believed in community care and did not believe in those large kinds of institutions. And he was delighted by this litigation. And I had him in class saying so to students of public administration."

But the perception of other participants remains that the commissioner can be taken as a prototype of the aggrieved and angry administrator. David Shaw comments, "When Gary Thorne was commissioner he and Governor O'Neill made it very plain they were going to dig in their heels. Thorne was of the older generation—he was a part of the old-boy network around the country. He was prevailed upon by many of his older colleagues to make a last-ditch effort in Connecticut, to dig his heels in, to fight tooth and nail. He announced very publicly and very firmly that he would never be a party to a consent decree, that he would litigate this right down to the last second, and that he would fight it thoroughly."

In the Boston housing case, the original tenants organization appears to have been a front for the housing authority. According to Paul Garrity, "There was an existing tenants union called the Tenants' Policy Council, which was so bad—it was really corrupt. They stole money, and after a couple of years of dealing with them, I ordered it defunded."

When Harry Spence became receiver, his position paralleled that of Brian Lensink, the present commissioner for mental retardation in Connecticut: both showed genuine sympathy and respect for the clients. Paul Garrity puts it this way: "Harry put a lot of time, trouble, and effort into developing a new citywide tenants' organization and also putting community organizers in the projects to tell people, 'You're worthwhile, you know. You are a good person. You should get out there and vote. You constitute more than 10 percent of the population of the city of Boston. That's a swing vote. And you can get conditions changed. You have the power, you know, to create a sense of self-esteem.'"

And Spence moved to build a genuine tenant organization, if only to escape being a captive of the plaintiff lawyers. "I think we actually looked upon organizing as means to political empowerment. But I have to say that, at the same time, I think there was another function for us of organizing the tenants which we fumbled a great deal, yet it saved us from being captive to the plaintiffs. The lawyers defined the interests of the tenants as they understood it. One of my problems was to avoid being a creature of these lawyers. They'd gotten the receivership they wanted, but it was also clear that if we served their interests directly all the time, we would lose the fundamental constituency of the tenants. By encouraging the genuine, real tenant organizations, which the plaintiffs could hardly object to, we broke out from under the thrall of the plaintiffs, because the political groups of tenant organizations took over, in essence. By making them more legitimate, the plaintiffs' hold on us was diminished. What actually happened was we used the decentralization theme to say, 'Wait a minute. We shouldn't be resolving these issues in a centralized, bureaucratic and legalistic way. These issues of public housing are real-life problems in real projects, and each project is different from another. We, at the housing authority, ought to be sitting down and talking with the tenants in the local projects.' Which we did. The effort was to build political capacity and to decentralize the problem."

However, even Spence's posture can be seen as manipulative, and John Moran expresses a view more typical of even the enlightened administrator. "In the early days, there was a prison reform group. My first meeting with them was after a month on the job, and three hundred attended. They didn't even believe I'd show up, but fully three hundred attended. At another meeting six months later, twenty showed up. Now we've come before a federal court, and no one attends, except representatives of the local American Civil Liberties Union and a couple of ex-inmates."

The resentment administrators are likely to feel at having the tables turned on them (at the "inmates taking over the nuthouse," of "amateurism running rampant") is a factor of fundamental importance in remedial law. Willis Hawley puts his finger on the difficulty in the colloquium's concluding discussion. "The problem, of course, is to change the behavior of people in the agency, and if that's the case, one can ask some simple questions. What are the motivations that people bring to the enterprise? Is that the problem? Or is the problem an absence of resources? Or is the problem an absence of competence? Competence, resources, and motivation are not unrelated, but as I worked through desegregation cases trying to ask these questions, I felt that the directions I came up with were fairly clear. If the problem's not fundamentally one of motivation, then monitoring is not a big problem. If it is, however, then the notion that we somehow rely on bottom-up solutions to solve the problem is, if you will, whistling Dixie—literally."

Target Agency Responses: (1) Obstructionism

In some instances, so great is an administration's shocked resentment at judicial intrusion that Robert Oppenheimer's metaphor of relations between the United States and the Soviet Union in the nuclear age—"Two scorpions corked in a bottle"—seems appropriate. As one sifts through Robert Whittlesey's four semiannual reports as first master in the Boston housing case, an indisputable record emerges of sabotage at all levels of the agency.

From an initial expression of concern that "the Board of Commissioners of the Authority is not fully committed to carrying out the purposes of the Consent Decree," Whittlesey's reports become increasingly detailed and infused with a tone of angry frustration. He pointed out that subplans are not being implemented, agreed-upon budgets are not prepared, and the board's inattention to housing conditions is close to gross mismanagement and incompetence. The master found that "the board has repeatedly failed to act expeditiously" and contests the master's and the court's rights repeatedly. Finally, a lack of cooperation by the staff with the master precluded any meaningful exchange of information between master and authority; senior staff made the implementation of mandated reforms "paper exercises." In his fourth report after documenting instance after instance of noncompliance, slippage of schedules for modernization and reform, failures to submit reports, and outright violation of the decree's personnel requirements, Whittlesey blew the whistle. He wrote the judge, "Our conclusion, not lightly arrived at, is that only through drastic change in both the BHA's method of governance and the agency's leadership will any significant progress be possible. In a word, action by this court has become the last, best hope for the survival of public housing in Boston."

If the Boston case represents what the city's local politicians call "being middled," in the finest expression of that art form, target agencies in other courts display similar dispositions, even if their tactics are not so skillful. In Rhode Island, Judge Pettine labeled the department's early behavior prior to Moran's appearance as "the ugly and shocking outward manifestations of a deeper dysfunction, an attitude of cynicism, hopelessness, predatory selfishness, and careless indifference that appears to infect, to one degree or another, almost everyone who comes in contact with the ACI and that the present administration, like its predecessors, appears powerless to correct or even arrest."

Willis Hawley describes the resistance the Compliance Assistance Panel found in Denver, over and beyond the aggressive tactics of the defense lawyers: "The board wouldn't play," and "the staff was running scared from the school board," and the result for a long time was stalemate. "While the judge can implement an assignment plan and a teacher plan, and so forth, and create the structures, what no judge can do, and in fact no school board can do, is to change the hearts and minds of the teachers and school principals and school board members, who in the long run are necessary to pull this off, because it's what is at the end of the bus ride that counts. It's not the bus ride itself."

Similarly, Brian Lensink describes the system he inherited in Connecticut and the steps required to change it. "The system, like many mental retardation systems, had been built on a very dictatorial and authoritarian approach to management, very internally directed. The average stay of a manager was something like twenty-five years. They were very much entrenched in the direction that they had been going, even though the previous commissioner had left. That's not at all atypical in a field like this. We felt that we needed to make some major changes in personalities, in organizational structure and approach, and, probably most of all, in philosophical orientation. And the only way to do that was to get in some new players and make everything else kind of off-balance for a period of time. You need to change the whole bureaucracy, the whole system, or I think that it will bounce back."

Target Agency Responses: (2) Technical Compliance

Outright obstruction and defiance seem to have their limits, even if they can be played out a long time and even if real change in philosophy and behavior comes hard, as Hawley and Lensink suggest. In the end Whittlesey blew the whistle, and Paul Garrity concluded "the agency was God-damned bad, and we just took it over."

Firing a recalcitrant public executive officer and hiring a new one has its limits, too, as Phillip Cooper points out. "There is a notion that somehow the court talks with the commissioner of an agency and this results in a positive outcome. That strategy flies in the face of what we know about bottom-up and top-down relationships of authority within organizations. Indeed, if there is one consensus about organizational problems, it seems to be the question, 'How do you deal with middle management?'—not so much top management, or even line-service providers. We might be able to use some of the literature which talks about authority positions, both top-down and bottom-up, and tie that to the question of how the organization then relates to a court which may, unfortunately, assume a unitary actor. There is an area in which I think we can inform the courts, by a discussion of the complexity of what appears to be a unitary actor."

More pungently, James Scamman describes the mind-set of middle management regardless of who the chief administrator may be. "A second response in agencies under court order is C.Y.F.—cover your fanny. When I walked in, I asked staff members what they thought. And they said, 'We think we want to do whatever you want.'

"There was a cut-and-dried approach to dealing with longevity in the system and promotion within the organization that did not support creativity, planning, or initiative on anyone's part. It was "protect your turf and cover your fanny," and if you smile and be nice you won't get in trouble and you can get promoted. People who had taken initiative in the past had either gotten caught in the political buzz saw or had been called up in front of the court to defend their actions and their decisions in a formal court setting, some of them having to face either lying about what they had done to protect themselves or overtly testifying against their superiors or against the school board, because they had tried to take some initiative. So they were not going to be exposed either way.

"I found that there was an enormous dual-level management of such simple things as data. We have impressive facilities for securing and massaging data. But we take care never to use them for staff counts, dropouts, grading patterns, what have you. Nobody can get any straight answers, and every time you get some information, it's conflicting with what existed before. I'm talking about the whole psychology of what happens when people are afraid either of their political bosses or afraid to expose themselves in terms of recognizing and admitting there are problems and recognizing that many of the best ways to solve those problems is take a proactive stance."

Robert Whittlesey identifies a variant of middle-management intransigence where it is coupled with an aggressive legal defense. He depicts the BHA's attorneys, with billable fees exceeding $500,000 during the negotiations in drafting the consent decree and overseeing its implementation, as "fronting" for a recalcitrant, uninformed, and incompetent board. After two hundred hours of negotiation, the court, the master, and legal counsels crafted a series of recommendations and procedural arrangements designed to establish "the rules of the game." But the authority's counsel insisted that the court rule on every interpretation of language in the decree and the language of each of the thirteen substantive plans.

"One of the last issues to be resolved was the extent of the board's responsibility for the consent decree. BHA's counsel stated that the BHA's position was that only the administrator would be bound by the consent decree. But counsel for the plaintiff class insisted that the board of commissioners as well as the administrator must be responsible for the decree's implementation, since the board has overall legal authority for BHA's operations. Eventually, BHA agreed that the board would be bound by the provisions of the consent decree. When the consent decree was formally presented to the board on April 27, 1976, it was adopted."

Thereafter, in the implementation phase, defendant's counsel, Choate, Hall & Stewart, consistently intervened to challenge the master's role. The firm protested the master's involvement in the search for and appointment of a new administrator and deputy administrator. Overruled by the court, it then objected to personnel requirements in recruitment of senior staff. When the deadlines for submitting critical subplans, such as work orders, were not met and the goals of vacancy management and affirmative action were not met, the defendant's counsel blamed the master. "On the basis of the virtual paralysis now upon the management division's capacity for staff training and planning because of non-subplan-related demands of the master's office, plaintiffs, and plaintiff attorneys, implementation of this subplan will not be possible until after the completion or suspension of the current court hearings."

Increasingly, senior authority staff failed to file plans (and when they did, they were often inconsistent), found it inconvenient to meet with the master's staff, failed to share information, failed to fill vacancies. The law firm had set the tone of resistance for the entire organization, encouraging middle management to evade or ignore consent-decree obligations in the belief their nonfeasance and misfeasance would be protected by counsel in court. In bureaucratic parlance, they "nibbled" the master's work to death. Thus, they set the stage for the more Draconian court strategy of receivership.

Target Agency Responses:
(3) If You Can't Beat Them, Join Them

Outright obstructionism and formal compliance coupled with informal sabotage are two patterns Vose participants identified not only in the four cases discussed but also in the wide range of cases in which they had collectively been involved. There is a third administrative posture, most usually adopted by administrators who succeed the original defendants in the case. This stance is one of embracing the court and its orders, using the court as justification for the reforms the new chief executive officer wants to bring about on his or her own initiative.

This strategy is most evident in the Connecticut case, and participants were quick to detect it. Alan Altshuler considers it to be an almost covert equivalent to receivership. "One would think that the more profound the organizational change, the greater the need for eventually the kind of receivership that Judge Paul Garrity imposed in the housing case. Yet in the mental retardation case, where it seemed that a fairly conservative approach was being pursued and the monitors were told to stay out of court and try to bring the parties together, a striking thing occurred: A former expert witness for the plaintiffs became the administrator of the agency. And so, while he was not officially a receiver, the chief executor of the agency came to be somebody who was in thorough sympathy with the court order."

Our Connecticut colleagues do not disagree. Their efforts are process oriented with the aim of bringing about comprehensive, systemic change—in David Shaw's words, "gently forcing the parties to work together." Shaw continues, "The court's approach throughout the roughly three years of implementation so far has been not to become directly involved in mandating change. The judge has held frequent status conferences, and he has tried his best to keep the court monitors between the plaintiffs, on the one hand, and the commissioner, on the other. And he's used that very successfully, in a very gentle way, to coerce change from the state without issuing a lot of mandatory injunctions. At some point, it may be necessary for the court to enter more coercive orders, but to date, significant change has been brought about by the system of status conferences and encouragement."

In sharp contrast to the detailed provisions contained in the 250-page consent decree of the Boston housing case, where the dotting of i's and the crossing of t's were the subject of prolonged debate, the brief Connecticut decree, in Ronald Melzer's phrase, "said basically, 'The monitors should monitor.' What few disputes we have had, have been primarily around means and not ends. While it does get tedious to have a group of people commenting on what an administrator would consider to be administrative prerogative, the litigation has a ratcheting effect on the progress that we are making. When you tighten something with a rachet wrench, the ratchet keeps you at least at the point that you've been before. Even though you may not get it any tighter, there's no likelihood of its slipping back."

But the key factor was the disposition of Brian Lensink, the new commissioner who had been in fact an expert witness for the plaintiffs, whose philosophy, shaped twenty years earlier, is grounded in the conviction that institutions are "devastating to mentally retarded persons." On his arrival Lensink found the monitors had "done a good job of educating the interim director, who then became my deputy." He embarked on an effort to bring about "broad" systematic change, even though he viewed the consent decree as "relatively narrow in applicability." Today he regards the process approach with its emphasis on education by the monitors and generally vague standards of quality assurance as clearly superior to receivership.

"I don't think you could put the department into receivership and get very far. I think you'd have to keep it there for an awfully long time, so you'd defeat the purpose of a quick change, and then give it back to the state. I'm absolutely convinced that this process is going to be another three years on top of the existing three years, and the real challenge is to figure out how the court can be effective in the process. I think Magistrate Egan has done a particularly masterful job of that. He's a gentle kind of person who doesn't let you get away with a thing. And he uses the monitors effectively as a buffer and also the experts, with a lot of different focuses."

Other participants question the "sweetheart deal" aspect of the commissioner's dual role—former expert, present administrator—and ask if in fact his "collusion" with the court constrained his freedom to do what he wanted to do." Lensink is clear as to the advantage he has: "I don't know that even today you can really say it's protection or collusion or even conspiracy. We try to set goals within the department. The goals have to be incorporated as state goals. When this does not occur, we often do not meet the goals. Now, you know, I want to meet the goals, and sometimes it is not just myself or our department who doesn't meet the goals, it's the state system. I certainly enjoy the court's assistance in helping the department meet its goals. Sometimes the department can't meet the goals, and it's not the rest of the state system that is at fault. It's all of us together. The total state system is often not doing as well as it should or could, and I think it would be disastrous if the court were not there. Until we have made a total change organizationally, administratively, and philosophically, the department would revert quickly back to its old ways.

"You should not conclude from my comments that there is no controversy. There are contempt motions, particularly when it is believed that individual class members are hurt in some way. Even though there may be some agreement philosophically, certainly when one of the class members is involved and the plaintiffs feel we are not complying with the consent decree, they go to court."

Lensink objects to any notion that he is not engaged in adversarial relations, or is engaged in "ugly" collusion, and he views the "quality assurance" role of the monitors as critical. Shaw emphasizes that the consent-decree process has marked advantages over the continued formal litigation, which "takes a tremendous toll on everyone involved" in terms of cost and time. Both resent the notion that they have conspired to balloon the department's budget at the expense of other public priorities.

Lensink replies "I am concerned about this impression that somehow the court case gave undue political power to getting something funded from the legislature. I've never had them appropriate everything that I wanted, even with a court case. And other agencies have similar court cases going on—the Corrections Department, the Mental Health Department, the Children's Services Department, and the Department of Retardation are all using their court cases to try to gain a little bit more visibility in the politicking and the process of getting money. To think that they somehow corrupt the political process in forcing legislatures to do things is incorrect. In fact, I think the judges have been incredibly frustrated as to how little and how impotent they often are in that part of the arena."

Shaw adds: "A number of commentators suggested that the result of these cases often was an appropriation of money that somehow deprived other needy groups of money. In my fifteen years or so of public-interest litigation, that is just not the case. These cases result in perhaps an increased appropriation to one agency, but I have never seen one group of people deprived of money because of litigation."

If the debate on administrative-judicial collaboration proved inconclusive, the strategy for administrators coming fresh on the scene is appealing. In Denver, James Scamman favors this approach. "In terms of how we get these things institutionalized, I absolutely agree; I have created my own compliance team. Internally, we have a compliance office. We have an outside advisory group that reports to me analyzing all of our data and information about our current status. And that is, in fact, working. It's not being public; we are not chastizing people publicly. People don't get their names in the paper and things like this, but change is occurring and progress is being made at all levels of the institution as a result of this proactive stance."

And Harry Spence concludes that whatever success he enjoyed as receiver turned on his ability to avoid formal litigation procedures. "I think the genius of the receivership solution that the judge decided on was that it allowed me to become intensely political. I didn't have to go in hearings before him once a week and explain what I was doing, as long as I could keep the plaintiffs happy. The plaintiffs could draw and quarter me if they could pull me into court, get me before the judge, and say we don't like what Spence is doing. But as long as I could keep the plaintiffs happy, no one could get me in court before him. No one could force me to translate the impossible of my categories of political and managerial thinking into this untranslatable other reality that was so different from the one I deal with. And in four and a half years I never appeared once in court, not once. I tried my best to stay out of there because I knew that court appearances would be fatal to my ability to do what I had to do for the judge and for the system and for the process."

Summing Up

The history of the cases and the broader experience of the participants suggest the ultimate futility of outright obstructionism to and surreptitious evasion of court mandate. Judges and their experts come to recognize both forms of affront to court authority and respond in the end with even more stringent requirements. But for the target agencies, collaboration or collusion by and of itself does not always bring success either in complying with the court or in preserving institutional integrity. There is, as Mark Moore and other participants continually remind us, a broader environment to be recognized and accommodated if the agency is to find some equilibrium as it struggles to reconcile the values of equity, effectiveness, and efficiency. To that world, the colloquium gave considerable attention.

Five   *The Big Picture*

It is convenient to think of the environment which surrounds the courts and the target agencies as consisting of at least two parts. The first is the general governmental system of which they are a component: the state or local executive and legislative branches. The second part falls under the broader and more elusive rubric "political culture."

Conventionally, political culture is defined as a collective psychological orientation toward government structure, incumbents in public office, and particular policies, decisions, or enforcement of decisions. Or, with a particular focus on the United States, Daniel Elazar has defined it as "the particular pattern of orientation to political action in which each political system is embedded."[1] Elazar goes on to distinguish among individualistic, moralistic, and traditional cultures in American states and localities, representing respectively a market-oriented, antipublic activist, patronage-prone disposition; disposition

---

[1]See Gabriel A. Almand and Sidney Verba, *The Civic Culture* (Boston: Little Brown, 1963), and Daniel Elazar, *American Federalism: A View from the States* (New York: Crowell, 1972).

to view politics as healthy and issue oriented; and a disposition which is essentially elitist and conerned with maintaining the existing order.

Vose participants were not especially concerned with pinpointing particular cultures for the cases considered. Yet their discussions do emphasize repeatedly that one can neither understand nor evaluate the play-out of remedial law without taking the environmental forces into account. Furthermore several participants identify judicial unwillingness or inability to factor in environmental variables as a crucial deficiency in the litigation and remedy phases of their deliberations.

The Governmental Settings

Target agency administrators are eloquent in making clear that their organizations are not islands of autonomy. John Moran knew the bigger picture when he was considering the Rhode Island post. "I went to look at the place, and I said, 'Well, I can work only with the governor. I've got to go talk with the governor.'"

He elaborates: "We have to deal with an unbelievable variety of public bureaucrats—the purchasing division, the state buildings division, the executive office, the legislative committees. We have spent more than a year trying to determine the site for a new medium-security institution. I'm not giving an excuse. Now I'm going to go back to the court soon, and the judge will say, 'Well, what happened to that year?' What am I going to tell him?

"Then we get into labor-management things. We get into contracts that have been negotiated over decades. We're talking about a civil-service system that restricts our flexibility to put the right people in the right place. We get one major middle-management opening, for example. We can only deal with the top three people. Virtually every position in the uniformed ranks is selected on a seniority basis. We have no ability whatever to assign people to particular positions. Correctional officers pick the unit they are going to work in, the shift they are going to work on, and the specific post they are going to work on. It's like being in major league baseball, you know. They fire the managers, but the players remain the same."

Brian Lensink echoes Moran's observations. "The other thing that I'm not so sure the plaintiffs always fully understand is how much a part other aspects of state government play in the process of change—

the Personnel Division and the Public Works Department, which are outside of our department, and, of course, the Office of Planning and Management is no small entity to deal with. The Department of Income Maintenance, which handles all the federal funds, and the unions, and the complexity of a nonunified parent constituency are all equally important hindrances to progress and affect the speed with which you would like to have change occur.

"It is important to remember that there are other major institutions that need to change at the same time you are changing this rather narrow Department of Mental Retardation. When moving out into a community you have to change the employment structure and medical structure so as to be more accepting. In this state, unfortunately, previous administrations have thrown a lot of people into long-term care facilities in hopes of avoiding litigation only to have it incorporated into the litigation. When you also have to deal with the nursing home industry, you have picked up a real challenge."

More than fellow state and local agencies are involved. Robert Whittlesey points out that for Boston public housing "most of the money comes directly from the federal government, so that the local administrators of public housing have a direct relationship with the federal government." He goes on to cite HUD's repeated and ineffective attempts to make the BHA reform and how HUD compounded, not eased, the task of the master.

Willis Hawley and David Shaw remind us that the federal government can be an actor, and a fickle one, in court as well. As Hawley says, "In 1981 a new administration came to office in Washington. The assistant attorney general for civil rights in the Justice Department has his own novel view of the Constitution and announced that the Keyes formula would no longer apply. Somehow or other, the Justice Department would decide that that was the case, and that the Reagan Administration was about to enter several cases around the country on behalf of school districts or defendants encouraging local resistance to the plan and stopping in midflight what had been one of the really successful efforts in the country." Shaw says that "the United States Justice Department came in and helped us litigate until the end, when they switched sides just at the time the case went to court, shortly after Ronald Reagan took over as president."

Listening to the administrators and court experts, Phillip Cooper sees the successful application of remedial law as an exercise in interorganizational as well as intraorganizational theory. "I have reference, in particular, to the literature on such matters as organizational learning. I think that that is one dimension in which we can operate. Because, indeed, it is an interorganizational arrangement. Up to now our discussion has been principally court-to-subject matter and court-to-responsible political official. But the big problem in remedy design and implementation is not the prison, not the mental health commission, but its relationship to the civil service commission, the management and budget office, and the others. There again, I think that interorganizational theory can help us somewhat."

Robert Katzmann follows up. "In terms of bureaucracies we should always recognize the desire for autonomy of bureaucracies and the resistance to coordination among bureaucracies. To the extent that you have many actors involved, as we do in these cases, obviously it becomes more difficult. One must look at the external factors that are necessary to maintain support for the remedy. That is, to the extent we are involved with legislatures, other outside bureaucracies, or bureaucracies which are not parties to the suit at all but may have bearings on the problems, we have a problem that is interorganizational in character. If we're talking about a school desegregation case, we may really be talking as much about housing or housing remedies as anything else. One must consider such external forces."

Don Horowitz would emphasize the heterogeneity of the immediate organizational environment of the beneficiaries as well as the formal actors. "In three of the cases that we considered, heterogeneity of the plaintiffs was readily apparent. In Denver there were Mexican-Americans as well as Blacks. In the Connecticut case there were two sets of parents. In the Boston Housing Authority case there were the actual tenants, and then there were those who nominally represented them, the legal services attorneys."

Of special note in the government system environment is whether the target agency is a line agency reporting to a governor or mayor or whether it comes with the policy apparatus of an elected lay board. The latter arrangement appears to complicate enormously the task of the administrator. In both the Denver and Boston cases, the politically elected or politically appointed board offered the most direct and unyielding opposition to the court—and this behavior pattern is documented time and again in the literature on school desegregation.

Two consequences flow from the interposition of the lay board between the court and the administrator. The first is that organizational compliance tends to be paralyzed, especially at the middle-management level by fear of board reprisal, as the earlier comments of James Scamman and Robert Whittlesey have made clear. "The board smothers bureaucracy" was the way the administrators characterized the situation. And reflecting on his new position in Denver as the court appears to back away, Scamman observes: "No one on the school board had ever been in circumstances in which they had to take responsibility for their own decisions to manage the system. They were there either early on, as pro- or antibusers, and then, more recently, as 'Let's get beyond that,' but not on a proactive platform about 'We ought to do this for the kids in our community.' So the school board itself is having trouble coming to grips with a basic philosophy on which five or six or seven members can agree and a program for the system that is proactive and long-range and is progressive down the road.

"All of a sudden now, with the possibility that the court relationship with the system may change, I'm viewed entirely differently. All of a sudden this business could be serious. This guy we hired might have some impact on the system, and he might even be here beyond the jurisdiction of the court. And there are not structures and philosophies in place to handle that. And so the challenge I'm facing right now is trying to deal with myself as a reality, as a person, where before I was a symbol of a chair."

Another dimension arises from the presence of the lay board—the opportunity it provides to let more visible and more powerful elected political figures off the hook. Paul Garrity's "druthers" in the Boston housing case "would be to have the housing authority be a line agency in the office of the mayor. The mayor of Boston, who ran for office in late 1983, said he would take the authority back. I had to beat up on him for ten months to get him to take it back. It still hasn't worked out. The mayor doesn't want it back." Neither did the previous mayor, as Whittlesey pointed out.

For political chief executives, involvement in programs under unpopular court order is most often seen as a no-win situation. As one participant put it, better to let "the pygmies that get on those boards play to the peanut gallery and take their cheap shots at the judge, than for me to try to act like a statesman." A case study by the John F. Kennedy Institute of Politics on the BHA makes clear that this was the consistent policy of Mayor Kevin White throughout the early years of the case.

The hands-off position of truly powerful political figures in a community robs target agency administrators and judges of more than just political support and leverage. It also diminishes the cooperation and help from other public agencies which are responsible to the political chief executive and take their signals from her or him. Governors, even presidents (as in the case of Gerald Ford and the Boston schools), can adopt a similar posture of indifference or outright disavowal, with traumatic effects on the executive agencies.

Yet without an intervening lay board, the "distancing" of elective officials with general authority is more visible and more subject to media and public commentary. The most difficult circumstances for the target agency administrator, the participants conclude, is to be enmeshed in the always complex network of interagency relations *and* have an elected lay board present—*and* have the court formally or informally oblivious to that fact.

The Political Culture: (1) The Clients

The second dimension of the environment poses even more problems for the administrator, however willing he or she is to follow the court directives and work toward genuine institutional reform. Two properties of political culture figure prominently in shaping a workable resolution to the problem of securing rights and achieving institutional mission. The first is the fact that the parties bringing suit and seeking redress of grievances lack general political clout. The second is that the public at large, or a vocal, politically potent segment of it, is opposed to the court's position.

The testimony respecting the absence of plaintiffs' power in the general political arena is substantial. Prisoners who cannot vote, minority parents, tenants "who don't know who their friends are," and families of the mentally retarded are not the stuff of powerful special-interest groups. Bronstein observes that "politicians and policymakers see no respectable constituency. To the contrary, it is good politics to suggest that you are treating prisoners even harsher and will treat them more harshly in the future."

Moran says, "I defy you here to name an individual who campaigned for governor on a platform of prison reform backed up by the necessary resources to bring it about. I know of one individual who did that, perhaps one of the best—and I've known a lot of governors— who was defeated as a result of that in the state of Delaware, namely, a man named Peterson. So it is not a political issue, it is not a priority. The public doesn't care. There is no constituency as there is for mental health or mental retardation or education."

Although proud of the work of CARC, Margaret Dignoti drastically discounts Moran's appraisal of the effectiveness of her organization. "We are a pretty tough group of advocates and are still intensely involved, but what was critical was the legal talent we had on our side—talent and integrity."

Indeed, one of the features of the Connecticut case was the split between two groups of the patients' families. Paula Caproni, who compiled the colloquium's case summary of CARC v. Thorne et al. (see Appendix 4), describes the initial hesitancy of CARC and the divisive role of the opposition group, the Mansfield Parents Association: "After a few divisive meetings, CARC voted to join the suit, but three local chapters of the CARC—Bridgeport, Stamford, and New London—left the group in opposition. CARC, because of its role as community service providers, was accused of using the suit for financial benefit. The state was accused of providing more assistance to ARC groups which did not support the lawsuit. Bridgeport withdrew $20,000 in membership fees when it withdrew its membership.

"The United Cerebral Palsy Association and Connecticut Society for Autistic Children chose not to join. Advocacy groups which were service providers as well as advocates for the handicapped were concerned that such a suit might 'bite the hand that fed them.' At that time, United Cerebral Palsy Association was getting money from the state. They later publicly supported the suit.

"The Mansfield Parents Association bitterly opposed CARC's efforts toward deinstitutionalization, claiming that the class action suit was not representing the will of everyone in the class. The members of the Mansfield Parents Association, primarily older parents with adult children who had been institutionalized for years, had invested much of their lives in maintaining and improving the quality of life at MTC. They were fearful that community placement might be detrimental to their children. The CARC parents and advocates were younger and had younger children. Having felt the benefit of legislation which had entitled their children to an education, and having had more experience with community support systems, they were more aware of the alternatives to institutionalization, had higher expectations of what their children could accomplish, and were optimistic about the possibilities for a community-based residential and service network for the mentally retarded.

"The divisiveness between the parties in the suit did not stop at the ideological level. Practical concerns—such as the cost of institutional versus community-based care—were used to support the parties' positions. They could not agree on the comparative costs of institutionally based and community-based residences for the mentally retarded."

In Denver, Scamman also doubts the capacity of advocate interest groups to sustain their position effectively without the continuing protection of the court. "There is no organized structure for decision making within the community that ameliorates the various pressures of special-interest groups who have been represented through the court but now find that the court may no longer be there. So we have minority communities that have heavily depended upon the plaintiffs to advocate their positions, and the court to protect them, that now may be needing to negotiate with a larger political system. And, frankly, those communication channels and structures are not in place. The parent groups are very school oriented but not district oriented."

And Scamman notes the policy positions of the interest groups change over time. "My sense is that there is no support, anywhere, in our community for continuing, or let alone expanding, transportation of students for racial balance purposes. I'm hearing throughout, particularly throughout our black community, 'What has happened when we can have black kids go all the way through school and never have a black teacher?' 'Where is role modeling?' Where is there a critical mass of support needed for keeping acculturation in place? Almost all of people from the community now are saying, 'Enough is enough.'"

In Boston, Whittlesey reflects that the tenants were "totally confused as to whom they should go to for help in the situation. Some tenants thought that their best friend was the board of commissioners—the very body that was responsible for their plight.

Indeed, so fragile and feeble do the interest groups often appear that Paul Garrity, the judge in the Boston housing case, became suspicious of the integrity of the plaintiff-lawyer-client relation. "I constantly pressed counsel for the plaintiff, 'Hey, are you really representing your constituency here? Are you really talking to tenants in the development? Are you sure you aren't off on your own toot?'"

Elaine Johansen sums up the limitations of the advocacy groups involved and substantiates Clement Vose's central finding that interest-group behavior is significant in the judicial arena. She ranks the relative power positions of interest groups by field in the following order: education, mental health, public housing, and prisons.

Her central proposition runs this way: "The further the enterprise is from effectively realizing a central value of the political culture, the less supported its work and organizational autonomy, and the heavier the external scrutiny. Societal values are acted out in the political system. Prisoners and the poor who inhabit public housing are seen as personal and moral failures in a country where social mobility is a civic religion. Political constituencies organized to project the legitimacy of the needs and worth of client populations in prisons and public housing have more difficulty building general public support or custodial agency sensitivity to civil rights than do supporters of education or care for the mentally retarded. Often client populations resort to fugitive activities such as rebellion, counterorganizations, and sabotage because they recognize that they are not only dispossessed but despised. Similarly, there is less sympathy toward or respect for organizational providers of these services. There is a hierarchy of public and political support for intervention roughly equivalent to society's values."

The Political Culture: (2) The Public at Large

If the interest groups which initiate institutional reform litigation possess few political resources outside the courtroom—if their objectives are substantially at variance with those of the general political culture—it is not surprising that the courts themselves appear to have gone "off the reservation" as far as the public at large is concerned. They undertake what Jonathan Sack calls "counter-majoritarian policies." They place in jeopardy what the Vose participants held to be "the moral authority of the court—its basic legitimacy."

Paul Garrity acknowledges the risk. "The sine qua non for a judge is not to be political but to be a good politician, and you have to walk that fine line between blowing your legitimacy as a judge and being political enough to affect the environment in which the organization exists."

Altshuler frames the dilemma this way: "To what extent can the judges, as part of their strategy of intervention, worry about building political support for their intervention? Presumably, other things being equal, every judge would like to build political support for his intervention and have his actions be popular as they emerge. But what we are seeing in these cases in very substantial part is the courts' performing a very critical traditional constitutional role, which is protecting weak minorities in a populist political system which has, for a variety of reasons over time, neglected the rights and interests of these weak minorities or aggressively contravened these rights, as in the segregation cases. It may well be that while there's a little bit of flexibility in that system to try to build political support, the courts are fundamentally at odds with the political system in these circumstances."

Following up, Kaplan is dubious about the court's ability to affect a political culture positively. "I question whether the courts are equipped to have a serious impact on the political culture of a local environment. And again, that's because courts, by definition, are not the philosopher-kings in this society. So, if we're talking about making sustained changes, I'm not sure courts are the instrument. The objectives of society change. The courts, for example, are unable to shape the current educational effort to put back more authority in individual school principals, on the basis of objectives concerned with the quality of education, even while the court still has jurisdiction. So the courts are sometimes unable to influence basic community changes with respect to educational objectives—even if they run counter to the assumed objectives of the courts themselves."

Yet, if the political culture is to be confronted, that challenge is a greater one than a recalcitrant bureaucracy. James Scamman makes this point: "Let me respond to the notion of bureaucracy versus politics of the basic society and take issue with the assumption that the real adversary is a bureaucracy. I don't believe so. I think it is the politics of the community, the basic values of the society; so I don't see adversaries to progress being the bureaucracy. I look at it in terms of the bureaucracy needing to respond to the politics of the community in order to stay on the horse. And that's true not only of the superintendent. That also goes down far deeper into the institution, the organization.

"The business community has, by and large, left the whole thing alone because it is afraid that you get your fingers dirty when you get messed up in court cases and desegregation. So there is no basic support group or power-structure support group within the community that says, 'This is what we want our schools to be.' I am dealing with the whole change in phenomenon that the removal or potential removal of the court as a viable force in the guidance of the district may cause a vacuum. It has some very serious proportion, and that's new to me and it's new to the community.

"The greatest danger as far as public opinion is concerned and the single most important problem in school desegregation (and I suspect in some of these other issues) is delay. It is delay and the uncertainty that parents hate. It is the major cause of white flight. People say, 'I don't know what school my kids are going to attend.' Delay is also a sop or bait to those who would resist the outcome, who believe that somehow or other if they just wait longer the judge will go away, or the current administration in Washington will come to the rescue, or whatever. You know, people are not very sophisticated about these matters. In Denver, I can tell you that the school board absolutely believed that if the Reagan administration entered this case, the federal judge would just cave in. And in fact, they imagined that the attorney general could tell the federal judge just what to do. You may think that's silly, and you could tell them differently, but the longer cases drag on, the worse it gets.

"In short, we're testing whether this remedy can be supported by the society at large. We are a democratic institution, and the remedies we bring about in solving our own problems basically have to be acceptable to the population or they'll excise the whole process and leave it, which we've seen happen."

The trick becomes one of transforming the political culture—in Mark Moore's words, "creating powerful political forces in support of the litigation." John Finger attests that it has been done, yet the way the transformation occurs remains elusive. "Where desegregation works best—North Carolina, for example—you find the leadership in the community taking the position to tell the positive war stories, to create the climate, because in fact people are ambivalent. They know it's a good thing to do this. Most of the kids are not having negative experiences, and so you need to tip the balance, change the climate. And, you've got to see the whole community as your culture.

"In Denver, we've gotten to the point where people are not saying, 'Let's turn the clock back.' We've gotten the positive plan so established that people want to maintain where we are. We need to do more, of course, to achieve higher levels of objectives within certain schools, and particularly the Hispanic populations. Within the black community people are saying we've done enough. That's what I hear. No one is saying turn it back and throw it away. We've gotten, at least to this point, where I think if we get out from under court order we will not have a community revolution to go back to the neighborhood school."

In struggling with "culture modification," the engagement of key elites, the manipulation of public opinion, and the propriety of judges as "politicians," the role of media commands attention, and their activities take on the dimensions of a two-edged sword. By awarding priority to a remedial law decision on the six o'clock news, front page, or repeated editorials, the litigation can become a "media event." Certainly the four cases reviewed here have been and continue to be. Paul Garrity observes: "It's absolutely essential to win the hearts and minds of the local media, both print and electronic, in order to deal effectively with the organizations that are involved in a particular case. A front-page horror story will position a judge in his or her reaction to the parties in that particular case on that particular day." Yet, public attention compounds the target agency's problems.

Shep Melnick comments on Paul Garrity's activism: "This type of publicity erodes public trust in government bureaucracies, making it more difficult for them to accomplish their goals. This touches on something very basic. Most advocates of judicial activism like government programs but express fear and loathing of government bureaucracies. The problem is that you can't have the former without the latter. Courts appeal to them because judges are part of the government but not part of the bureaucracy. They are the 'libertarian' authority. To the extent that judges are expected to make bureaucracy acceptable to those who reject authority, they are bound to fail."

Summing Up

Courts and target agencies are in hot water most of the time as remedial litigation proceeds. Their immediate environment, those parts of the general governmental system which are affected by the litigation, is not well disposed toward them. Governors and legislators who respond to the priorities of court-ordered reform receive few if any brownie points from the electorate. Other agencies and departments, especially oversight budget and management agencies, find their own priorities upset and often see courts diverting resources from other departments with equally compelling needs and far more public support. If the target agency is unfortunate enough to have its own "political" governance by a lay board or commission, the temptation to "cut and run" from judicial mandate is powerful indeed.

Even more threatening to the success of institutional reform litigation is the political culture—the orientation of the majority of activists in the political system. The general citizen is likely to regard the clients served by the site-specific organizations as undeserving and their representatives as agitators, demanding special privileges and acquiring special status by taking unfair advantage of the judicial process. They are seen as crybabies, unwilling to abide by the existing rules of the game, always appealing to the umpire. When the media discover "the story," the court's authority may be momentarily enhanced, if the journalistic interpretation of the case is a sob story of unfair, brutal, and inhumane treatment. Still, the impact is not likely to be long sustained; it flops like yesterday's newspaper under the table. The bureaucracy involved will be excoriated, but in the end, the judge's moral position will be put at risk, and he or she will be seen as yet another example of the imperial judiciary.

Nonetheless, the original stipulation stands. Remedial law is here to stay. Are there better ways in which its processes can be shaped? Are there preferable strategies for fashioning remedies? Most important of all, when and how can courts get out? What are the conditions for cloture?

Six

When Will It Ever End?

"We're like a fish out of water—a fish can live out of water for a little while—but if he doesn't go back in once in a while, he will die." So conclude the deliberations of the Vose administrative panel. Grant that there are overwhelming justifications for courts' engaging in remedial law and engendering controversy. Attorney David Shaw, a participant in the Connecticut case, observes: "Before judicial involvement, the political process for not insubstantial parts of the population was highly unresponsive. The institutions could hardly be termed democratic, and the system displaced may not be worthy of respect or defense." Grant, too, that the court's moral authority, its legitimacy, can be more impaired by a hands-off policy than by involvement. In Shaw's words: "The weakening of authority as a consequence of remedial complexities must be compared to the weakening if courts abandon their equitable powers. Shrinking from the paramount issues of the day could do more to undermine the judiciary's credibility than has getting entangled in administrative processes."

Nonetheless, at some point, the judicial restorative process must end. That is one conclusion to which all Vose participants, at least in theory, subscribe. The urgent task now, as Vose participant Marcy

Murninghan, an expert on judicial intervention in public schools, points out, is establishing "the conditions of disengagement," establishing a commitment by "all the actors to cloture," verifying "the capacity of the institution to manage itself," and asserting "the credibility of the institution not just to the parties primary to the case but to other actors, to community groups, to the media, to the legislators. Does that system have any integrity in the eyes of the bystanders?"

Without cloture, Robert Gilmour reminds us, "we will never face the issue of accountability. Surely, we have some notions, not just in organization theory, but in democratic theory about the accountability for the administration of public agencies funded by citizens with public funds. Ultimately we have a notion that we elect those who will then appoint administrators and that there will be an accountability ultimately to elected officials, including legislators, who are going to appropriate monies. The issue is inescapable: should judges be determining how the public purse is to be spent, how the agencies conduct their operation?"

Otherwise, James Scamman warns, "the mission of the institution can be unalterably changed or accidentally changed." Without cloture, Shep Melnick warns, "There is something terribly wrong with what the courts are doing, reinforced by fears that the judiciary, supposedly the most thoughtful of the branches, has not given much thought to what it wants to do."

So Alan Altshuler posits the ultimate goal: How can we assure that "judicial intervention serves as an effective catalyst for the emergence of favorable bureaucratic support systems for arrangements that are basically more fair, more in concert with the constitutional tradition of the United States?"

Or, by what means do we achieve Mark Moore's optimistic scenario—"When you put the spotlight on these institutions and you force them to perform in one area, people begin to ask how they are performing in a wide variety of other areas. Politically, as well as judicially, they ask these questions, and it may be they end up performing better on a wide variety of indicators simultaneously."

So the end of agency restoration is clear—but by what means? The sticky wicket of *how* to reach the promised land remains. Here, Vose participants do not display consensus, or anything approaching it in the sense of a grand design. Herbert Kaufman concludes that "the question of timely cloture is probably unanswerable. Everyone at the colloquium agrees that judges should strive to disengage themselves as soon as possible, but that's certainly laboring the obvious. If the administrators can convince the courts and the complaining parties that the new arrangements will continue even if the courts terminate active supervision, the question would answer itself. But that would give suspicious litigants a veto over judicial withdrawal. I guess the agencies just have to keep petitioning the courts to surrender power. Some will have better luck than others."

Al Bronstein is even more skeptical. "It is fruitless to spend time talking about how to achieve cloture in institutional litigation. I waited for the bolt of lightning here, as I spend a good deal of my time in meetings dedicated to (1) ideas for expediting implementation, (2) getting the court out of the problem, and (3) ending the litigation. It never ends unless the lawyers sell out. The 'cures' will come only when there is a radical restructuring of our society. Until then we must keep suing the bad guys."

Still others are not disposed to accept an indefinite, inconclusive, case-by-case approach to court withdrawal. Adopting the fish-out-of-water analogy, they see organizational atrophy as the inevitable result. Robert Katzmann argues, for example, that "while it is unrealistic to think that standards for cloture can always be stated at the outset, such criteria can be devised at a later point. The process, I envision, would involve two steps. First, the court makes a ruling about liability, about rights. Certainly, the declaration of rights is an important—indeed, vital—part of the American experience. It would not necessarily, at that point, delineate in sharp detail the remedy. The court, at the liability juncture, would begin the remedial process by asking of the parties, 'How can the wrong be remedied,' requiring that each remedial option submitted to the courts include an organizational analysis. That is, what would the world look like at the end of the remedial process? What means are required to achieve that last step? The court would then choose among the options, taking into account organizational efficacy. At that point, it could then declare unambiguously what would constitute cloture. This approach may have the virtue of building public support for the remedy—in advance of the judicial decree of the remedy itself."

Harry Spence concludes that such a process of withdrawal is essential. "On the cloture issue, the judge and I had a number of discussions about how one brought it to an end because the judge, Paul Garrity, is democratic in the eighteenth-century sense, a real democrat, and was constantly offended at his own role as an elitist. I think a couple of things were clear. First, you couldn't wait until everything was cured. Second, when the conditions have changed sufficiently that whatever progress hopefully occurs under the receivership can realistically be expected to continue, that's an appropriate point for the court to get out. As long as the democratic political process is reasonably carrying out its duties and meeting a reasonable standard of performance, the court ought to get out right away. Fair statement? We were there to start momentum, not to arrive at final solutions, to create the conditions that would allow continued progress. But we could not supplant the democratic political process for longer than the period necessary to reestablish the enabling conditions for the democratic process to fulfill its legal obligations."

But what is "reasonable process," "sufficient momentum," a viable "democratic process?" Vose participants offer two approaches to answering these questions. The first is a checklist of operational requirements derived from the generation of remedial law experience. They are essentially tactical, professional improvements which the present record shows to be obviously necessary. The second involves establishing the conditions appropriate for choosing between two major alternative strategies, what Altshuler terms "minimalist" and "maximalist" approaches, usually dependent upon whether or not the violations discovered are narrow or broad. Melnick calls them the "war of attrition" and the "blitzkrieg" strategies. Both approaches deserve inspection.

Dos and Don'ts in Remedial Law

Plainly, as the colloquium reviewed successive phases of the litigation process for institutional reform, opportunities for substantial improvements appeared—common-sense changes which require little or no elaboration of organizational theory. Melnick and Katzmann take the lead in identifying improvements which go substantially beyond marginal adjustments in judicial and administrative behavior.

Melnick emphasizes the importance of establishing the goals of a case as lucidly and explicitly as possible—the rights violated which are to be secured. He warns about a judicial tendency to carry forward a set of "latent" rights alongside of more formally articulated constitutional rights and particularly to subsume their consideration in the remedy phase of the litigation. His understanding of the position of many judges, experts, and litigants is that "at rock bottom there wasn't much agreement on what rights were violated, and much of the discussion of remedies was really discussion about what exactly are these rights. Let me give you a couple of examples of that. Superintendent Scamman said that the goalposts keep moving, which indicates to me that somehow our understanding of what rights are keeps changing. John Finger said that Judge Doyle at one point said, 'What we are trying to do here is to provide the best possible education for children.' That's different from what I thought was the stated goal of many of these desegregation cases, which was to provide racially nonidentifiable schools. That's quite different from providing the best possible education. Both are important goals, but it's not clear to me that they are both either the same thing or compatible.

"In the Boston housing case the original violations, which were very serious ones, involved health and safety violations, but later it became clear that one of the chief goals of the court and of the receiver was to regain some amount of desegregation. Paul Garrity asserted that the ultimate goal of this litigation was 'to politicize and empower the poor.' The Connecticut case said, 'Overall the decree did not focus on detail; instead it focused on the process.' One aspect of that case was trying to decide what extent of deinstitutionalization you want to have. The remedy basically was trying to go back and say, 'OK, let's have a process for working out what we think the right is in the first place.'

"According to this approach, exemplified by Abram Chayes's works, rights really evolve in this process of negotiation, trial and error, and experimentation. I think that's wrong. The more one could put in the very beginning of the process, to be clear in writing an opinion, the more one meets a basic tenet of public administration, which is, 'Know your goals.' Try to have your goals as operational as you can at the very beginning. Don't view the process of finding remedies as the process of operationalizing your goals.

"Spell those goals out. The more that you can spell them out in the beginning, the better off you're going to be. The traditional concepts of constitutional law and of spelling out rights in the beginning are quite compatible with the precepts, as limited as they are, of public administration. You should try to think in advance what resources are going to be necessary to meet this goal. You should define goals in a way that you are going to have a chance of carrying them out. In short, behind all the rhetoric is a very deep disagreement about the nature of constitutional rights which judges are alarmingly unwilling to acknowledge. When the goalposts keep moving, the case will never end, and whatever good is achieved, the case will be declared a failure by the plaintiff.

"I believe forcing judges to be more specific about the nature of constitutional (or even statutory) rights has several advantages: (1) It provides judges with performance standards; (2) it forces judges to define goals, rather than allowing them to delegate this crucial task to self-declared 'experts'; (3) it encourages judges to determine early on whether a particular right is one which the court can actually guarantee, or whether its vindication requires action well beyond the court's control; (4) it gives appellate courts more control over trial courts; and (5) it gives judges a way to decide when to get out."

Robert Katzmann pushes even further. Confirming the need for unambiguous goals, he goes on to emphasize organizational means. "One way to think about whether goals can be achieved is to focus, in an ideal world, upon the final stages. How do we want the world to look at the end of the process? We should determine what means are available to achieve that desired end, knowing in advance, of course, that there may be so many unanticipated consequences that we can't say with any certainty how that end will be in its precise form. In identifying the means, or some of them, we could look at such things as the mission, the goals, the power structure, the task structure, problems of autonomy and coordination in terms of restructuring organizations, thinking in terms of a checklist of things to consider. Here, I draw upon my 1980 *Yale Law Journal* article, 'Judicial Intervention and Organization Theory.'

"With respect to mission—a mission can be thought of as a distinctive and valued set of behaviors, a shared feeling among organizational personnel about the nature of feasibility and importance of the organization's tasks. We should understand that to the extent an organization has the sense of mission, it will be difficult for courts to change it. One should think in terms of the resources as well that would be needed to

change the mission of a particular bureaucracy or the several bureaucracies involved. One must also think in terms of who's in the
bureaucracy. Are they professionals whose behavior and policy perspectives are constrained by norms derived from external reference
groups that allocate rewards such as advancement and esteem? Those
are particularly likely to resist attempts to reorient the organization in a
way that conflicts with the conception of what the bureaucracy is
doing.

"Another thing to look at is the power structures of the bureaucracy
or bureaucracies involved. That is especially important at the district
court level. Once you get to the court of appeals level, you may not have
the time to undertake the inquiry that's required. It's important to
understand what part of the bureaucracy you're trying to effect, to
whom you are vesting leadership roles. If a judge is going to try to effect
change, he or she should at least try to have a sense of the limits of his or
her opportunities.

"Also, it may be useful to look at the tasks involved. Are we talking
about tasks involving a lot of discretion, or are we talking about tasks
which are routine, where it's easier to monitor what's going on? That
also will affect, I think, the nature of the judicial involvement. Then we
should always recognize the desire for autonomy and the resistance to
coordination among bureaucracies. Finally, we must look at the outside forces necessary to support the remedies."

To the admonitions to clarify goals and make explicit any hidden
agenda within them, and to achieve as professional a grasp as possible
of the true nature of the bureaucratic beast, the administrators add four
other items: time, sensitivity to the public impression, open communications, and sensitivity to second-order consequences. Katzmann continues: "There needs to be adequate time to prepare the understanding
of the issues and to prepare the resources and to allow the change that is
desired to occur. There just simply must be enough time.

"Do not underestimate the necessity of maintaining what is called
the high side of public relations. When you get involved in litigation
like this, it creates all kinds of publicity and tends to erode the confidence of the public in the institution, no matter what the problem is.
You are inevitably involved in a question of image, and people don't
make informed judgments—they simply know if you're in the paper,
something is wrong. And then the whole thing gets broadbrushed.

"We also feel that the court, the judge himself or herself, should have first-hand information, should go out and physically walk in the footsteps of those who are trying to bring about the change, get firsthand information. The normal sort of courtroom procedure of having evidence submitted, having cross-examination knowledge filtered through the attorneys, simply isn't enough. The judge must personally have a feel for what's going on. The normal rules of communication cannot apply as strictly here as in other cases because you have the possibility of a much higher level of error rate. We need to try to make sure that the plaintiffs' investment in the solution isn't the only one, that the court itself comes to a conclusion in its own head about the direction that it's important to go. And that's going to require some real firsthand, eyeball-to-eyeball, hands-on, 'talk-with-the-troops' kind of feeling."

Trying to anticipate second-order consequences proves especially important to administrators. James Scamman illustrates the point: "Because the formula was insisted upon by the plaintiffs and the judge, we had to pull out a twelve-year senior black teacher from a very small elementary school in a predominantly Anglo area who had become the most popular teacher in the school, three weeks after school started, simply to have that school be in compliance. We also spent a half day in court arguing whether you round the bottom of a range up or down depending upon whether it's .4 or .5 percent. When you get into that kind of specificity on a staffing ratio, or when you get into that kind of specificity on student transfers of whether a 1 percent change in a school student population by virtue of a hardship transfer constitutes an integrative or a segregative transfer by definition, you've gotten beyond the point of keeping the broader goals in sight. You must know the impact that these decisions will have on the mission of the organization and whether it can maintain its ability to serve its major purpose. I was proud to hear from John Moran of Rhode Island that one of the alternatives he didn't look at was turning all the prisoners out on the street in order to lower the number of prisoners—although we lost thirty thousand students and went from a two-thirds Anglo district to a one-third Anglo district during this period.

"Our board has adopted a policy that if any school is to move five points away from the mean, the school will develop an impact statement, an environmental-impact kind of statement of the educational reasons, the racial and ethnic projection, in order to try to make sure that it is not getting into problems again. And what is the impact on student capabilities and their chances for success? For example, we have at Manual High School a virtually all-white honor society in a two-thirds black school. That's unacceptable. I was their dinner speaker; that's how I found out about it. And, are we going to continue to have basically all Anglo faculties with increasingly minority school districts?"

Throughout the colloquium additional tips on effective behavior appear. Participants generally applaud the spirit of informality that pervaded the Boston housing case, such as Judge Paul Garrity's informational breakfasts with Harry Spence, even though the Massachusetts Supreme Judicial Court looked askance at this deliberate violation of the traditional rules barring communication of parties in the case with the judge, except in the courtroom. They continued to worry about the process by which experts are chosen, noting Ronald Melzer's chance stop "in a rest area on one of Vermont's two highways to take a call from Commissioner Lensink." They view as fortunate Melzer's knowing the other monitors. ("The state didn't know anything very much about the other monitors. I happened to be the only person who knew everyone else, and I thought we could work together.") But they judge such a selection process to be dubious. They remain concerned about the ideological commitments experts may carry. (Robert Wood discovered early in the Boston school case that the experts there viewed their aim—and so declared themselves in print *after* the case moved into its final stages—to be to "empower" the parents and the teachers.) They believe, that despite the unsettled state of organizational theory, some knowledge of its proverbs is helpful to experts, lawyers, and courts.

Most of all, participants identify the quality or competence of all the actors as critical to more successful resolution of the dispute. At the same time, mindful of Arthur Garrity's warning that "judges are not fungible," they acknowledge the inability of any power to assure competence of court, plaintiff, counsel, and administrator. They wish, of course, for the appearance of leaders—charismatic, catalytic agents. "I suggest," observes Marshall Kaplan, "that in Boston, Harry Spence's competence and leadership were probably as important as the institutional mechanism of receivership." But most confess organizational theory provides few guides as to how to find leaders in timely fashion.

Nonetheless, the participants argue for the actors being self-conscious about their extraordinarily demanding duties. And they are insistent that no court, under the claim of simply proposing "curative" remedies, be oblivious to the organizational consequences.

Blitzkrieg or War of Attrition?

The checklist just enumerated can go far to help the remedial law process "shape up" and perhaps signal clearer criteria for cloture. It does not relieve the courts, however, of the choice of remedies, of strategy, in the context of the target organization and its environment. Should courts intervene incrementally over time, patiently, in "minimalist" fashion, or should they adopt the "maximalist" approach of radical surgery? More precisely, under what conditions are the two strategies—or some mix of them—best advanced? Altshuler comments: "We've seen cases like the school cases in which the particular problem, although thoroughgoing in its effects, was one that was susceptible to statistical remedy. You identify particular indicators and say, 'Deal with those indicators,' having to do with racial balance in the school population, by school, and in the teacher, administrative, and employee populations. There was not a need for total transformation of the educational process or of the central mission of the schools, only a question of how people mix as they avail themselves of that process.

"On the other hand, we saw three cases where it was a totality of conditions or at least a broad range of violations identified simultaneously in the system. It led to the view that really a total system transformation was required. As one looks at the prison case, the case of the institutionalized mentally retarded, and the housing case, one is talking about the total mission of the institution, an extraordinarily poor performance with respect to that mission on a wide variety of indicators. Clearly, the broader the range of violations, the more thoroughgoing they are as it relates to the mission of the institution, the more profound the assault on the existing organizational structure that seems called for.

"The first obvious, but not necessarily true, interpretation that emerges is that it is very hard for the 'minimalist' approach—simply issuing orders that relate to the particular violations and crafting them as narrowly as possible to negate the violations—to work in 'the totality of conditions' situation. I understand that when Bob Wood was school superintendent he asked his counsel whether there was any possibility that he and the school department were in violation of any of Judge Arthur Garrity's orders. His counsel responded that there were about 405 orders at latest count and that he scarcely had time to count them, let alone read them to figure out whether the schools were fully in compliance. So there comes a point at which the 'minimalist' approach tends to overwhelm the capacities of the system to respond, particularly if the system is really resistant and requires thoroughgoing change.

"This brings us to the debate between the virtues of short, intense intervention versus a more lengthy, distant, minimalist approach on a month-by-month basis, but one that perhaps becomes maximalist when looked at in a historic context if it has to go on for very long periods of time. On the one hand, we are concerned that long interventions tend to atrophy the political process around the institution, build up political resistance, and enervate the process. On the other hand, short and intense interventions may be insufficient to build a set of cultural expectations and inertial forces that a lengthy intervention extending over many years may bring about. That is, it may be that while there is resistance month by month in that situation, by keeping the pressure on over many years, the whole culture gradually begins to respond. There's time for new political generations to come to power who are not as defensive as the original political forces, not just in the agency, but in legislatures and in the larger political system. The institutions may not be transformed overnight, but they develop habits of doing things over a period of a decade or more which by inertial forces may continue into the future. Which is the better solution in a particular case, we are unable to say."

Complicating the issue of mini versus max are the social and political responses that neither court nor organization can easily anticipate or certainly control and which go beyond the unintended consequences the administrators identified. Altshuler addresses this matter. "One other issue is the problem of a slow-moving regulatory system versus a dynamic social system. Regulatory systems find it very difficult to move quickly enough to keep up with the inventiveness of the regulated parts. In school desegregation cases, for example, the school systems gradually respond to the judicial decrees, but meanwhile the people who prefer segregation are moving out of the central cities and are re-segregating themselves in a societal sense. Here judicial intervention is virtually powerless to deal with the social facts of the case, where the only intention is the intention of individuals who have moved to segregated communities and taken advantage of preexisting jurisdictional arrangements as opposed to governmental entities having taken direct segregationist action.

"In the case of public housing, it's possible to intervene to improve the upkeep and the expenditures on an existing public housing stock, but the public housing program dies while this is going on, in part, because of concerns about courts' requiring integrated public housing projects. Prison administrators respond to pressures to improve the conditions in the prisons, with respect to overcrowding, for example, while other courts under great political pressure are sending more and more people to the jails. With even larger expenditures, prison administrators can't keep up with the dynamically changing situation.

"Central question: Are the courts, as regulatory institutions (fundamentally, we're looking at a set of regulatory systems even more powerful and more legitimate than other regulatory institutions) profoundly disadvantaged in dealing with some dynamic aspects of the situation by the fact that, unlike other regulators who try to maintain freedom to operate case by case, the courts articulate principles? And do the principles (even though there is a bit of a moving goalpost phenomenon) become fairly stable points around which those who want to evade the regulations can operate and can get out from under the regulatory system?"

While Altshuler remains evenhanded in his analysis, the prospects of "social evasion" incline others to favor the blitzkrieg. Harry Spence argues that "if you understand the way in which organizations work, and the dynamics of organizations, one thing becomes absolutely clear: minimum intervention at each point in time assures ultimate maximum intervention; minimum intervention at any point in time always assures that you'll need to intervene a little more—the minimum is never enough. The dynamics of an organization are such that you need to affect so many things simultaneously to change the culture. The minimum intervention which only pushes two of the buttons of the twenty you need to push will assure that you need to push three more, and then three more, and then three more, and in the end you are going to be intervening everywhere. I would argue that the state court was able to intervene in a receivership far less. We did minimal intervention because we intervened massively, briefly. The problem of minimal intervention is in definition. What's minimal?"

Accepting without comment the observation that he seemed to be a direct descendant of Joseph Stalin on his mother's side and General Patton on his father's, Judge Paul Garrity comments: "I knew receivership was the way to go within a month after the housing case was filed, no question in my mind. But I had to wait four years to build a record before I could impose a receivership. There is no question in my mind that Judge Pettine, in the Rhode Island case, was wrong by not taking it over when he said, 'What do I do?' And there's absolutely no inhibition upon federal judges legally, if the gradualist approach doesn't work, to go in and take it over. Because if the gradualist approach doesn't work and you stay in continually in a gradualist mode, it's a prescription for impotency.

"Also, in school litigation, it's my firm belief that what needs to happen when a federal court intervenes is to find out what's coming down. And then set your standards. And if they don't comply with those standards, go in there, take it over, establish that unitary school system, do it for about two or three years, and then pull out. Now in Denver you've got a heel-dragging board of education, which has been going on for at least 15 years. What happens in a community when that takes place is that the public education system becomes totally divorced from that community. There is no longer any political support for public education in that community. That's what's happening in the cities in this country. And I don't care whether you have a good mayor and a lousy board, or a lousy board and a good mayor—the result's the same. Find out what's coming down. Tell them to fix it. Give them time to fix it. If they don't fix it, don't screw around with them. Take it over and fix it yourself, because you have the authority to do it as judge. And then pull out. And I stress again, the system loses all political legitimacy in a community if you don't do that."

The more extreme options continue to trouble some participants. For Don Horowitz there are serious questions on its impact, not just on the target organization and its political environment, but on the consequences for the court. Horowitz reminds Paul Garrity that he was chastised by higher court for his ex parte communications with Spence and his unconventional arrangements in the consent decree. Arthur Garrity observes that such precedents are very few for federal courts and the likelihood of reversal very high. The concern of both is that judicial impartiality is impaired, that no one is in court "pushing you to make sure you're not biased," and that that critical, however intangible, quality of moral authority is likely to be impaired, the very foundation of legitimacy. Paul Garrity concedes these are difficulties, but concludes: "I think there's an equal threat to illegitimacy or the morality of courts if the court fails. A court is asked to intervene and is not totally result oriented. I mean, a court is asked to intervene to get people to comply with the law because all else has failed. If the court fails here, I think that probably doesn't help the court's image too much."

Closing in on Cloture

Suppose we stipulate that the remedial litigation process can be "shaped up" in significant ways. That is, goals are specified with the precision Melnick, Katzmann, and Altshuler call for; the organizational capacity of the target agency is assessed as Scamman and Murninghan would have it; the actors are in fact competent; and all the other preferred conditions in handling media, anticipating second-order consequences, establishing open communications, etc. are in place. In other words, like an economist's wishful vision of the marketplace, we hypothesize a "model" remedial-law process.

Can we offer further counsel to specify the circumstances in which one or the other major strategies are most appropriate? Furthermore, can we indicate which of Cooper's formal remedies—process, performance standards, or specified discrete actions—work best? Further still, can we suggest the comparative advantages and liabilities of the judicial devices of continuing oversight from the bench or through monitors, consent decrees, and receivership?

From the Vose deliberations three variables emerge that seem dominant and most relevant: the extent of the violations, narrow or broad; the capability of the target agency, high or low; and the disposition of the political culture, supportive or hostile. Granting that the range in values of each variable is considerable, nonetheless a rough typology appears, ranging from the worst-case scenario of many violations, very low organizational capacity, and extreme cultural hostility to the best-case scenario of few violations, high organizational capacity, and supportive culture. The three dimensions can be most effectively depicted on a flat surface as they are in figure 1.

Eight cells appear in figure 1, and in each an appropriate remedy suggests itself: *Receivership* in the case of a hostile culture, where there are many violations and low organizational capacity; *consent decree* with an emphasis on process where there exists a supportive culture, few violations, and capable organizations; *direct oversight* with performance standards or specific actions when the culture is apathetic or tending toward hostile, violations are few, and organizational capacity is low. There is no arbitrary assignment of "best remedy" to each cell—judgment calls are necessary when values tend toward the mean for all variables. For example, what is best in the case where there are considerable violations (but not a situation approaching, in Bronstein's term, totality of conditions), a mediocre, run-of-the-mill organization, and an indifferent culture? Perhaps strict oversight with performance standards, but not receivership at the outset, and probably not a consent decree.

The utility in categorizing remedial law situations is certainly not in precise calibration of remedy to condition, in the legal sense. It does, however, suggest with some clarity the circumstances of clear *mismatch*. It helps explain the tortuous path of the Rhode Island litigation and the apparent success to date of the Connecticut consent decree, where the present dominant actors seem to share the same philosophical stance. It illuminates the stop-start character of Keyes, where two judges have presided over the case, and process and performance standards seem to have become entangled. It highlights the successive phases through which the Boston housing case moved—and the finality apparently achieved.

It is questionable whether the probabilities of cloture can be estimated by this typology, but as an explanation of why cloture has *not* occurred in so many remedial law cases, it appears to be more powerful. Courts have simply failed to identify consciously and deliberately the organizational and cultural variables which are present. Therefore, the "curative" remedies do not often prevail. Conscious, explicit efforts toward seeking a convergence of remedy and instruments to match organizational and cultural realities would at least enhance the pros-

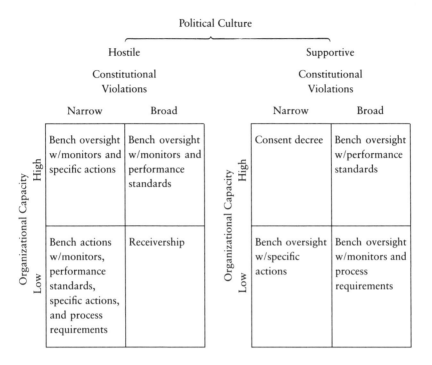

FIGURE 1. Variables Affecting Cloture

pects of cloture. Failure to consider these factors promises judicial frustration and failure.

From Organizational Theory to Political Theory

However the issue of cloture is resolved, one final dimension of remedial law processes requires commentary. Vose participants are acutely aware that the generation of institutional reform litigation took place simultaneously with a sea change in American politics and its social structure. After the turbulent sixties, the ground rules of our political behavior and the characteristics of our polity were shifting massively in the seventies and eighties. The judicial process was often at the eye of the storm, and one simply cannot evaluate its performance in the area of litigation with which we are concerned without taking that sea change into account.

Harry Spence characterizes the phenomenon this way. "Let me talk about the issue of diversity because I think the issue of race and the things that came out of this country's struggle with the issue of race is at the heart of each of these cases. The issue of race, I say, because each of the groups we're dealing with—whether they involve issues explicitly of race, prisoner issues, issues of poverty in public housing, or schools— race and the classes of people overlap in fair measure (perhaps less so in the mental health area).

"I think the civil rights struggle greatly informed notions about a couple of things. First, that the culture needed to tolerate much greater diversity and not put away in boxes people who differed from the majority, whether in race or problems of mental illness. And second, out of the civil rights struggle, a deep mistrust arose about the use of governmental authority because of the history of the abuse of that authority. A libertarian push arose, if you will, which maintained that the government can exercise its authority only when it can prove through a quite elaborate process certain very rational things, often in a highly elaborated and intellectually complex process.

"The result was a wide range of challenges to the authoritarian manner in which we have treated minority groups of all kinds in this country. The result was also a paralysis of government, of those agencies of government that dealt with those rules. The problem of governing in these new circumstances, with these new sensitivities, became vastly more complex and difficult than it was twenty years ago. Far more difficult because there were no simple rules. Far more difficult because you couldn't apply governmental force and sanctions with the simplicity and brutality frequently used before. Fundamental to all our deliberations is the issue of diversity and the complexities of governance in situations of diversity.

"Let me point to some of the organizational implications of diversity. In public housing, prior to the civil rights struggle, a housing authority could decide it didn't want single mothers—they were bad people. You couldn't have a criminal record. If you had any record of drug dealing or drug addiction, we don't want you. A whole series of categories were viewed as nefarious.

"The civil rights struggle brought a dramatic end to that and said, 'Absolutely not!' Those categories have been used as covers for racial segregation, particularly as a cover for keeping blacks out. So all of a sudden an agency that had just been used to writing rules was now being told that rule making was far more complex. You've got to start with the fact that we've had a diversity of cultures, of class, racial, and ethnic cultures. You've got a harder task there. You've got to figure out how to reconcile these interests and do it much better. Agencies collapsed. Their confidence to respond collapsed in the face of those demands.

"Centralization was a frequent response to the problem of the agency that had to deal with the possibility that its line people were engaging in racial and other forms of abuse. You say, 'No one can make a decison in the field. Everything has to come to the central office for review because I've got to make sure my lawyers have seen what you are doing because I'm going to have to defend it now, and make sure it fits my seven categories that I've been told by the court I have to fit.' So I centralize. The result is disaster because it totally ignores the fact that you have a reality of community life in a local area. It treats a housing program as though it were like a welfare program, as though it were not a life of people in a community but instead a bureaucratic system with papers and numbers to be manipulated. Alongside centralization came a vast increase in middle-management levels because of the documentation of all sorts of things that had never been documented before.

"Finally came the appropriate resistance to the application of governmental sanctions without very, very strong reason, whether that governmental sanction is eviction in public housing, institutionalization for a person who is mentally ill, or discipline in a prison system.

"Each of those things, growing out of changes in the sixties and seventies, produced paralysis in agencies, really right at the nexus of those problems. And we looked to the courts to break the logjam. It was natural to turn to the courts (since it was only they who finally had spoken the truth about race in the first place) and to look to them for solutions. What we're seeing are efforts to grapple with how one governs in a circumstance of diversity. We can no longer assume everyone shares a WASP middle-class set of assumptions of how the world ought to work. We can't apply those standards as governmentally mandated. We have a far more difficult and complex task of doing it in a diverse society. The courts' efforts, for all of their constant failures, represent enormously important opportunities to experiment with how that can happen, how to find new models for doing that, and how to rescue the agencies that have collapsed in the face of those challenges and, at least, give them a renewed opportunity to try to comprehend and an increased competence."

Spence's eloquent account of the new environment which public organizations and courts inhabit suggests a new judicial status, a status certainly not neutral in the conflictual world of diversity, perhaps quite beyond strict definitions of constitutional value, and committed, in Mark Moore's phrase, "to producing a substantive value."

Judge Arthur Garrity confirms that commitment is "so different from what it was only twenty-five or thirty-five years ago because we're no longer an American melting pot. That's gone out of style. We're now a society that is pluralistic from the bottom up. And as a society we wish to be sensitive to the rights, not just of racial-ethnic groups, but minorities of all sorts who were never even identified as recognizable groups ten years ago. That's the challenge of American society as I see it today, to vindicate the rights within the limits of the power of the officials of the various agencies involved. Not just the administrative agencies but, of course, the courts, which are also an agency of government. We probably need brand new beginnings in this whole area.

"Derrick Bell, who is a professor at the law school at Harvard, has an article called 'The Civil Rights Chronicles,' in the November 1985 issue of the *Harvard Law Review*. It's a bucket-of-cold-water-in-the-face type of approach. And he proposes that all of these remedies to secure the rights of minority groups, all of the nostrums, aren't going to do the trick. The change in the composition of the Supreme Court won't do it. And improvement in the economic conditions of this country will not do it. Self-help programs won't do it. He says there has to be a voluntary, purposeful, surrender by the establishments to which all of us belong of some of their power to the disenfranchised and relatively disenfranchised minorities in this country. Only if a broader approach to these problems is set in motion are these apparently intractable problems going to disappear."

James Breeden, a longtime civil rights leader in Boston and the director of Judge Arthur Garrity's monitoring council, adds: "Just to discuss court/school or court/institutions relations isn't enough. A whole set of relationships has to be taken into account—the rather peculiar things that happen because of an underlying social movement, or underlying set of changes going on in the society. The courts are just

one tool, and particular efforts such as school desegregation are challenging as a tactic in a larger effort for change. Abstract language that
deals only with one set of organizations and institutions seems to me to
squeeze out the important element of making some assessment of
where we, as a society, are in terms of social improvement or progress.
That frame of reference it seems to me is critical. I was telling Judge
Garrity that I would have quoted Derrick Bell, but I wouldn't have
footnoted it. I would have taken the responsibility for it myself."

To which no Vose participant seems to have entered a dissent.
Whatever the problems leading to selection of target organizations,
however clumsily judges have applied or misapplied remedial law,
whatever the frustrations of achieving cloture, no one doubts the signal
importance of the courts' broader political purpose and effect. None
gainsay that in the clear absence of effective executive and legislative
response to the new society, the courts must fill the political and policy
vacuum.

Appendix 1 *Palmigiano* v. *Garrahy* United States District Court, District of Rhode Island

Case history prepared by Daniel R. Pinello

Summary

Amid a national tide of prisoner unrest and court-ordered reform of state penitentiaries in the early 1970s, inmates at the Rhode Island Adult Correctional Institutions (ACI) at Cranston organized a mounting protest of intolerable living conditions there. The effort culminated in a 1977 federal court order directing massive changes in the facilities operated by the five-year-old Department of Corrections. Significant, though halting, improvements resulted at the ACI in the late 1970s. However, following withdrawal of federal subsidies in 1981 and a dramatically increasing inmate population directly linked to harsher judicial bail and sentencing behavior, substantial retrenchment occurred at the ACI in the early 1980s, resulting in further federal court intervention after 1984.

District court judge Raymond Pettine characterized the Department of Correction's approach to inmate care as responsive at best, with little or no ability or inclination to plan for institutional needs or change. During a decade-long struggle to transform the ACI, the court found that constant judicial monitoring of the department was necessary to achieve and maintain meaningful progress.

Chronology

March 11, 1970. New regulations for governing disciplinary and classification procedures at the ACI promulgated and adopted by the court as an interim eighteen-month decree.

April 5, 1972. First formal meeting of the National Prisoners Reform Association (NPRA) held at the ACI, attended by six or more inmates.

May 9, 1972. Court issued temporary restraining order and preliminary injunction to allow NPRA to continue meeting within the ACI.

December 18, 1972. Court prohibited prison officials from summarily barring law students, working as paralegal assistants to defense lawyers, from access to inmates in the ACI.

April 2, 1973. Prisoners at the ACI rioted.

May 10, 1973. Committee of prison officials investigating April 2 uprising issued its report, calling for general improvement of prison facilities.

May 27, 1973. Inmate at the ACI stabbed to death.

June 22, 1973. Prison guard at the ACI murdered by an inmate.

March 8, 1974. Court issued permanent injunction against suspension of the "Morris Rules," adopted in 1970.

July 1974. Inmate Nicholas Palmigiano commenced *pro se* federal court action alleging violations of the Eight and Fourteenth amendments.

June 1975. Federal cases involving the ACI consolidated, and attorney Mann appeared on all plaintiffs' behalf.

August 1975. Amended consolidated complaint served alleging a class action on behalf of all prisoners at the ACI.

July 23, 1976. Court certified class of plaintiff prisoners.

November 1976. J. Joseph Garrahy first elected governor of Rhode Island.

August 10, 1977. Court issued opinion and order in favor of plaintiffs' claims. (A summary of this order appears in the narrative following this chronology.)

August 1977: Governor Garrahy directed that no appeal of the August 10 order be taken and appointed an implementation team therefor.

October 27, 1977. Court appointed Allen F. Breed as special master.

November 1977. Governor Garrahy made statements to the press criticizing the actions taken by the federal court.

December 1977. Court issued letter acknowledging political tensions in the case.

December 1977. Governor's implementation team dismissed.

January 1978. Governor Garrahy requested some $300,000 from the legislature to implement order of August 10, 1977.

February 6, 1978. Only thirty-seven out of more than five hundred inmates had appeared before the prison Reclassification Board pursuant to the August 10 order.

February 10, 1978. Deadline set by court for defendants' reclassification of all prisoners at the ACI.

February 22, 1978. Defendants submitted to the Court (1) a "drawn-down" plan (i.e., to reduce the maximum-security inmate population to comply with the order of August 10, 1977) that projected an eventual total of 511 sentenced, male, classified offenders in the ACI, and (2) a plan for building a prefabricated industrial structure (named the Butler Building) adjacent to the medium-security facility to house vocational and work programs, with completion of construction scheduled for December 31, 1978.

1978. Legislature rejected governor's budget request and placed issue of prison-reform funding as a bond referendum in the general election.

March 28, 1978. Court found defendants had failed to comply with the reclassification of inmates ordered August 10, 1977, held defendants in civil contempt, and imposed daily fine of $1,000 for further noncompliance after May 1, 1978.

May 10, 1978. Delayed deadline set by court for defendants' full compliance with direction in the order of August 10, 1977, to create various rehabilitation programs for inmates at the ACI.

May 1978. Defendants obtained federal funding for the Butler Building from the Law Enforcement Assistance Administration.

1978. Allen Breed named director of the National Institute of Corrections, withdrawing as special master; J. Michael Keating, Jr., appointed to replace Breed.

July 12, 1978. Court found defendants' medical services at the ACI in substantial compliance with the order of August 10, 1977.

July 18, 1978. Court granted defendants a delay in compliance with the order of August 10, 1977, threatening sanctions for further noncompliance of "a substantial daily fine" or "possibly placing the ACI in receivership to bring about compliance with the August 10 order."

August 1, 1978. Delayed deadline set by court for defendants' compliance in establishing rehabilitation programs at the ACI.

August 4, 1978. Defendants informed the court that the Butler Building would not be ready for use realistically until February 1979.

August 7, 1978. Defendants submitted to the court a second "draw-down" plan, projecting an eventual total of 570 sentenced, male, classified offenders in the ACI.

August 1978. Defendants obtained possession from another state agency of the so-called "B" Building for minimum-security inmates.

September 15, 1978. Delayed deadline set by court for defendants' compliance in establishing rehabilitation programs at the ACI.

September 1978. Inmate leaders at the ACI transferred to the Federal Bureau of Prisons.

October 1978. Court granted defendants' requested extension for completion of the Butler Building to February 1979.

November 7, 1978. Rhode Island voters defeated prison-reform bond referendum.

November 9, 1978. Court found defendants in compliance with the programming requirements of the order of August 10, 1977 for the general sentenced inmate population of the maximum-security facility, but not so with regard to pretrial detainees in maximum and all prisoners in the medium-security facility. The court set specific plan and implementation deadlines in 1979 for the balance of defendants' compliance with the order of August 10, 1977.

December 15, 1978. Defendants opened bids from contractors for construction of the Butler Building.

December 1978. Ground broken for a new Intake Services Center to house up to 168 pretrial detainees at the ACI, with completion scheduled for August 1, 1980.

January 10, 1979. Special master issued year-end report revealing that a new high-security ("Supermax") facility housing 96 inmates was being built at the ACI, that a new building for housing rehabilitative programs for medium-security inmates was scheduled for completion in September 1979, and that the old maximum-security building would no longer house inmates as of September 1980.

January 25, 1979. Defendants signed construction contract for the Butler Building, requiring completion of the structure by August 26, 1979.

February 1979. Court awarded attorneys' fees of almost $120,000 to plaintiffs' counsel, to be paid by the state.

March 30, 1979. Special master found defendants in compliance with court's requirement to provide sentenced offenders in the maximum-security facility with meaningful full-time programs.

May 1, 1979. Defendants submitted to the court a third "draw-down" plan, projecting an eventual total of 574 sentenced, male, classified offenders in the ACI, and for the first time proposed formally indefinite retention of certain portions of the old maximum-security facility.

May 1979. Legislature and governor approved $449,000 for prison repairs and renovations, and the Law Enforcement Assistance Administration issued a matching grant.

June 19, 1979. Special master issued his eighteen-month progress report to the court revealing that defendants were seeking a reprieve from final condemnation of all the old maximum-security facility, that defendants wished to house approximately seventy protective-custody and maximum-security inmates there indefinitely, that defendants had not installed an objective classification system of inmates based on risk factors, that defendants were in full compliance with the mental health services and drug abuse treatment provisions of the order of August 10, 1977, and that full compliance with the balance of that order realistically was still eighteen to twenty-four months away.

September 1, 1979. Court-ordered deadline for completion of construction of the Butler Building, housing work and vocational programs for medium-security inmates.

November 11, 1979. Fully 42 percent of the sentenced male inmate population of the ACI remained classified as maximum security, compared to the national average of 22 percent.

November 24, 1979. A major inmate disturbance in the Behavioral Custody Unit (BCU) of the ACI caused widespread destruction of toilets, sinks, and beds in the unit.

December 3, 1979. Defendants submitted to the court a fourth "draw-down" plan, projecting an eventual total of 619 sentenced, male, classified offenders in the ACI. The court found defendants had failed to comply with the court-ordered deadline for completion of the Butler Building, held defendants in civil contempt, and imposed daily fine of $1,000 for further noncompliance after December 22, 1979.

December 1979. Date estimated by defendants in summer 1979 for completion of new Supermax facility.

December 31, 1979. Delayed deadline set by court for total closing of old maximum-security facility.

January 21, 1980. Court found that defendants had not provided an acceptable plan for reducing the maximum-security inmate population at the ACI and gave defendants until May 1, 1980, to submit a final draw-down plan to the court.

March 1980. First Circuit Court of Appeals affirmed award of attorneys fees.

1980. Legislature appropriated $451,000 for physical improvements of portions of the old maximum-security facility at the ACI.

July 29, 1980. Rhode Island voters defeated $5.83-million bond referendum for expansion of the Supermax facility at the ACI.

September 18, 1980. Special master issued findings of fact and recommendations to the court, revealing that defendants had no fixed written plans to close down any portion of the old maximum-security facility, that the total estimated cost for bringing all of the old maximum-security facility into compliance with minimum health and safety code requirements would be almost

$5 million, that defendants' total expenditures on renovation of that facility since the order of August 10, 1977, amounted to more than $1,500,000, that physical conditions in no area of that facility met the standards imposed by that order on other facilities at the ACI intended for permanent use, that programming in maximum security continued out of compliance with that order, and that the classification system implemented by defendants was in compliance with that order.

November 19, 1980. Court ordered that cellblocks A-B-C, D-E-F, and P-Q-R of the old maximum-security facility be closed forever in July 1981, that cellblocks M-N-O be closed forever unless the defendants provided a plan for their retention within thirty days and had money in hand to complete interim repairs by July 31, 1981, that cellblocks G-H-I and J-K-L (BCU) be closed down by December 31, 1984, unless they were brought into compliance with minimum health and safety standards, and that the Office of the Special Master cease to function on a regular basis by January 15, 1981.

November 1980. Date estimated by defendants in summer 1980 for completion of new Supermax facility.

January 1981. Supermax facility first occupied by maximum-security inmates.

May 1981. Legislature appropriated $450,000 for improvements in cellblocks M-N-O and P-Q-R of the old maximum-security facility.

July 1, 1981. Date estimated by defendants in summer 1980 for completion of new Intake Services Center.

September 1981. Daily average number of pretrial detainees at the ACI reached 184, a 90 percent increase over one year.

October 6, 1981. There were 206 pretrial detainees housed at the ACI.

October 29, 1981. Special master issued his quarterly report to the court, revealing that the defendants intended (1) to postpone opening the new Intake Services Center until July 1, 1982 in order to cover the deficiency in the Department of Corrections' 1981–82 budget, (2) to divert the $450,000 appropriated in May 1981 for cellblock improvements to the Department of Corrections' budget deficit, (3) to delete approximately sixty personnel positions throughout the Department of Corrections, including some required by the order of August 10, 1977, and (4) to terminate many rehabilitative and vocational programs at the ACI.

January 4, 1982. Court denied defendants' motion to modify dates ordered on November 19, 1980 for closing of the old maximum-security facility, ordered cellblocks A-B-C, D-E-F, M-N-O, and P-Q-R be closed down permanently upon completion of the Intake Services Center, and allowed cellblocks G-H-I and J-K-L be retained in use until 12/31/84.

January 15, 1982. Date estimated by defendants in fall 1981 for completion of new Intake Services Center at the ACI.

March 1982. Date estimated by defendants in winter 1981 for completion of new Intake Services Center.

November 1982. Rhode Island voters defeated $8.5-million bond referendum for prison reform.

November 1982. Legislature budgeted $412,746 for "Phase II" renovations of the maximum-security facility at the ACI.

September 16, 1983. Court awarded additional attorneys fees of almost $35,000 to plaintiffs' counsel to be paid by the state.

1984. Defendants commenced the double-celling of inmates at the Intake Services Center.

May 1984. Governor's Task Force on Overcrowding at the ACI stated that "prison overcrowding is becoming an increasingly alarming problem."

November 19, 1984. Court granted defendants an extension of time to June 1, 1985 to complete renovations of the old maximum-security facility and to July 1, 1985 to provide certain programming opportunities at the ACI.

July 22, 1985. Special master issued report showing that defendants were not in compliance with certain provisions of the order of November 19, 1984.

July 1985. Defendants commenced the triple-celling of inmates at the Intake Services Center.

January 3, 1986. Court enjoined the triple-celling of inmates at the Intake Services Center.

May 12, 1986. Court issued opinion and order finding that defendants remain in noncompliance with the order of August 10, 1977. (A summary of both such orders appears in the narrative following this chronology.)

Introduction

Published in 1958, Gresham Sykes's *Society of Captives* offered a graphic, sobering view of inmate life in an American maximum-security prison. Within a few years, Sykes's work became a standard reference in the professional literature advocating prison reform. See, for example, "Beyond the Ken of the Courts: A Critique of Judicial Refusal to Review the Complaints of Convicts," 72 *Yale Law Journal* 506 (1963), a law note which ended by quoting this thought with approval: "Judges spend their lives in consigning their fellow creatures to prison; and when some whisper reaches them that prisons are horribly cruel and destructive places, and that no creature fit to live should be sent there, they only remark calmly that prisons are not meant to be comfortable; which is no doubt the consideration that reconciled Pontius Pilate to the practice of crucifixion."[1]

[1]Quoted from George B. Shaw, *The Crime of Imprisonment* (1946), p. 14.

At the time of Sykes's investigation, federal courts traditionally had confined the Eighth Amendment prohibition against cruel and unusual punishment to discrete cases of excessive physical brutality inflicted by prison officials. Not until the late 1960s did federal circuit courts of appeal begin to emphasize nonphysical aspects of punishment in a correctional context as being within the amendment's ambit.

Holt v. *Sarver*, 309 F.Supp. 362 (E.D.Ark. 1970), was a judicial breakthrough in that the district court there was the first to declare, in a class action, that an entire state penitentiary system constituted cruel and unusual punishment. A veritable flood of similar inmate claims followed in the 1970s.

The professional literature stepped up criticism, enlarging its focus to deplore legislative inaction.

It is as controller of the purse that legislatures have had the greatest opportunity to aid prison reform; in that role, too, they have failed. Nationwide, less than $1.5 billion was appropriated to prison systems last year [1970]—a fraction of the sum appropriated to the police sector of the criminal justice system. Moreover, ninety-five per cent of the funds allocated to corrections go toward physical custody and confinement of prisoners, building maintenance, and salaries for custodial guards. Only five per cent remains for prisoner "upkeep"—health, social services and general rehabilitative programs.[2]

History in Rhode Island before Litigation

In October 1969, Rhode Island Legal Services sought a temporary restraining order and preliminary injunction on behalf of its inmate-clients at the ACI, requiring the defendant prison authorities to provide prisoners with certain hygienic, recreational, and religious services. After extensive court-supervised negotiations between the parties, new proposed regulations for governing disciplinary and classification procedures at the ACI were agreed upon by the litigants and adopted by the court as its interim decree for a trial period of eighteen months. *Morris* v. *Travisono*, 310 F.Supp. 857 (1970).

In 1971 and early 1972, Larry A. Schwartz, an employee of the Providence Corporation (a private, nonprofit, antipoverty organization) and chair of the Committee on Corrections of the Cooperative Area Manpower System (a governor-appointed committee overseeing various job-training programs throughout Rhode Island), and four members of the Rhode Island Junior League met with inmates at the ACI to discuss formation of an organization

[2] "The Role of the Eighth Amendment in Prison Reform," 38 *University of Chicago Law Review* 647, 649 (1971) [footnotes omitted].

ultimately named the National Prisoners Reform Association. By April 1972, organizational meetings of NPRA had been held at the ACI with at least six or more inmates participating. NPRA's goals were to improve prison conditions and to make people outside of the prison aware of conditions within. Inmate Nicholas Palmigiano was elected president of NPRA.

After initially allowing several meetings of NPRA, Director of Corrections Sharkey prohibited any further NPRA gatherings in the ACI. NPRA sued on First Amendment grounds, and Judge Raymond Pettine issued a temporary restraining order and preliminary injunction against the prison authorities to allow NPRA to meet within the ACI. *National Prisoners Reform Association* v. *Sharkey*, 347 F.Supp. 1234 (1972).

In 1973, ACI officials summarily barred law students, acting as paralegal assistants to defense attorneys, from entering the ACI. Judge Pettine then enjoined such conduct because it denied effective assistance of counsel. *Souza* v. *Travisono*, 368 F.Supp. 959 (1973).

On April 2, 1973, prisoners rioted at the ACI, causing substantial property damage to the facilities. On May 27, 1973, an inmate was stabbed to death. On June 22, 1973, an inmate murdered a prison guard.

As a result of these events, prison officials suspended the so-called Morris Rules, adopted from the 1969 litigation. Subsequently, Judge Pettine issued a permanent injunction against the suspension of those regulations. *Morris* v. *Travisono*, 373 F.Supp. 177 (1974).

Pertinent Data Attendant to Litigation

As of November 1974, the ACI housed 588 inmates, 448 (76.2 percent) of whom were white and 140 (23 percent) of whom were black. (See exhibit 1 for a graph of the inmate population at the ACI from 1971 through 1983.) The total annual expenditure at the ACI for the fiscal year 1975–76 was $7,521,438, amounting to $34.25 daily cost per prisoner.

As of April 1976, the racial composition of inmates at the maximum-security facility was 312 (76 percent) white, 84 (20 percent) black, and 12 (3 percent) Spanish-surnamed. At the medium-security facility, 90 (73 percent) were white, 32 (26 percent) black, and 2 (12 percent) Spanish-surnamed. These percentages remained relatively constant throughout the 1970s.

As of September 1976, the personnel at the maximum-security facility consisted of 145 male correctional officers, 134 of whom were white, 10 black, and 1 "other." At the medium-security facility the 73 male correctional officers comprised 66 whites, 6 blacks, and 1 "other."

By April 1977, the National Prisoners Reform Association was publishing a monthly newsletter, *NPRA News,* and distributing it nationally from within the ACI.

The Decision to Litigate

In July 1974, inmate Nicholas Palmigiano, appearing *pro se,* commenced a federal court action in forma pauperis against the governor of Rhode Island, the warden of the ACI, and its resident physician, alleging violations of the Eighth and Fourteenth amendments. An assistant attorney general of Rhode Island served an answer on behalf of all defendants. In November 1974, plaintiff himself conducted depositions of the warden and resident physician.

In June 1975, Palmigiano's case was consolidated with that of other inmates, and attorney Robert B. Mann appeared on behalf of all plaintiffs. In August 1975, an amended complaint, alleging a class action and adding the director of the Department of Corrections and the ACI's senior classifications officer as defendants, was filed. In September 1975, Richard A. Gonnella of the Inmate Legal Assistance Program joined Mann as plaintiffs' counsel, and Ronald A. Dwight, designated a special assistant attorney general, appeared on defendants' behalf.

In December 1975, Gregory C. Benik, special assistant attorney general, appeared as additional counsel for defendants. In June 1976, William Granfield Brody, special assistant attorney general, substituted as defendants' lead counsel, joined by the chief and assistant legal counsel for the Department of Corrections. Mr. Brody remained lead counsel for a substantial time thereafter.

By the time of the court's 1977 order, the parties to the consolidated actions were as follows:

Plaintiffs. Five prisoners of the ACI and the National Prisoners Reform Association, on behalf of all prisoners incarcerated at the ACI. The plaintiff class numbered over 650, including both pretrial detainees and sentenced prisoners.

Defendants. The governor of Rhode Island, its director of corrections, the warden of the ACI, and selected other prison officials.

Plaintiffs' claims. Violations of the Eighth and Fourteenth amendments and various provisions of Rhode Island state law.

Plaintiffs' grievances. Inmates housed in the ACI suffered constitutionally intolerable levels of fear and violence. Moreover, they lived in constitutionally intolerable conditions of confinement, which included gross filth, unsanitary living quarters, unsanitary food services, dangerously inadequate medical care, and near-total idleness. In addition, pretrial detainees were subjected punitively to conditions worse than those suffered by sentenced inmates. Prisoners in protective custody were also subjected to conditions worse than those suffered by sentenced prisoners.

Defendants' answer. General denial.

1977 Court Findings of Fact and of Law

In August 1977, after a two-week trial, Judge Pettine issued a lengthy opinion and order[3] resolving plaintiffs' claims, which holding is summarized as follows.

Findings of Fact

The maximum-security facility. Over 420 inmates were housed in a hundred-year-old building designed for 55 inmates, which facility was extremely filthy. Moreover, its plumbing was unsanitary, inadequate, and an imminent danger to public health. Heating and ventilation also were inadequate. For example, the January midday temperature in the facility reached only fifty degrees Fahrenheit. Furthermore, numerous fire hazards existed in the facility, and the food-service operation was an imminent public health danger. The infirmary failed to meet minimum standards for the control of infectious disease. In sum, most expert witnesses at trial could find nothing good to say about the facility.

The medium-security facility. This depression-era building housed 160 prisoners. Although not quite as bad as in the maximum-security facility, conditions were not much better.

The classification system. The system of classification of prisoners at the ACI was incapable of fulfilling any of the rehabilitative functions mandated by state law and was inadequate under any minimum standards. Inmates received no psychological or psychometric examinations, except in emergency cases. No written procedures existed to structure the classification process.

Medium security had disappeared as a classification status. Rather, the medium-security facility was used to house protective-custody inmates. True medium-security prisoners thus were sent to the maximum-security facility.

The effects of overclassification of prisoners permeated the entire system. For example, the director of classification was hesitant to grant inmates minimum-security status, since the change was so great, and as a result, the long wait to change classifications was a direct cause of a substantial portion of violence at the ACI—no real incentive existed for prisoners to stay out of trouble.

The failure of the classification system prevented any serious long-range

[3]443 F.Supp. 956.

planning to improve the ACI. No administrator had reliable data regarding exactly how many maximum-security cells were needed for high-risk inmates.

The defective classification system engendered the rampant violence and endemic fear of violence existing at the ACI. That is, victims were not separated out from predators at the ACI. The specter of rape among prisoners was ever present. Moreover, so-called protective custody was little safer than maximum security.

An inadequate force of guards also contributed to prison violence and fear of violence at the ACI. Inmates existed in a state of constant violence and fear, and it was impossible for defendants to provide adequate protection to inmates at the ACI under the then-present classification system.

Program and idleness. Idleness in the ACI was the central fact of existence for nearly all inmates in medium and maximum at nearly all hours of the day. It bred boredom and a quest for excitement and was a major cause of violence. Opportunities for inmates to work were wholly inadequate by any minimum standards. Very few educational or vocational-training opportunities existed for prisoners. Grossly inadequate recreation facilities or programs for inmates exacerbated matters at the ACI.

Pretrial detainees. The number of pretrial detainees varied from 120 to 175, although the awaiting-trial cellblock in maximum could house only 99 inmates. Constant daily contact existed between pretrial detainees and sentenced prisoners. Pretrial detainees were exposed to conditions worse than those suffered by sentenced inmates in either maximum or medium.

Drug abuse and treatment. Illegal drugs were available and used extensively inside the ACI, and they were a substantial cause of violence among inmates. At least 70 percent of all prisoners were using such drugs, and at least 50 percent were drug dependent. The ACI's facilities for diagnosing and treating drug abuse were wholly inadequate. In fact, much of the drug trafficking originated with the prison guards. The ACI medical staff had no formal protocols for the withdrawal or treatment of heroin, barbiturate, or polydrug users, nor even commonly understood unwritten policies.

Medical care. The system of medical-care delivery at the ACI was inadequate by any accepted standard to meet the inmates' routine and emergency health care needs. The defendants consciously disregarded a grave and substantial risk to the health and well-being of the inmates entrusted to their care, in the form of the needless occurrence, prolongation, and exacerbation of serious injury, illness, and suffering. The psychiatric and psychological evaluations and treatment were inadequate to meet the needs of the inmate population.

Summary findings of fact. The institution was unfit for human habitation. Inmates were subjected to constant fear and violence. Rehabilitation was impossible. Rather, dehabilitation—the mental and physical deterioration of inmates—was inevitable at the ACI.

The maximum-security building had long outlived its usefulness.

A complete absence of effective leadership and management capability on the part of the responsible state officials existed. The management of the ACI was basically incapable of creating a safe, orderly, and hygienic prison to accomplish the state's twin goals of custody and, where possible, rehabilitation.

Findings of Law

Defendants' conduct violated several provisions of Rhode Island statutes as well as the Eighth and Fourteenth amendments.

Although acknowledging that *Procunier* v. *Martinez,* 416 U.S. 396 (1974), cautioned federal district courts to be wary of interfering with the operation of state prison systems, Judge Pettine relied on numerous circuit- and district-court precedents, in addition to Rhode Island statutes, as authority for his action.

Officials who engage in massive, systemic deprivations of prisoners' constitutional rights are entitled to, and can expect, no deference from the federal courts, for the constitution reserves no power to the state to violate constitutional rights of any citizens. *Newman* v. *Alabama,* 349 F.Supp. 278 (M.D.Ala. 1972), *aff'd in part,* 503 F.2d 1320 (5th Cir. 1974), *cert denied,* 421 U.S. 948 (1975); *Gates* v. *Collier,* 501 F.2d 1291 (5th Cir. 1974); *Williams* v. *Edwards,* 547 F.2d 1206 (5th Cir. 1977); *Pugh* v. *Locke,* 406 F.Supp. 318 (M.D.Ala. 1976). Nor can lack of funds, or invocations of the virtues of the legislative process, excuse constitutional violations or judicial default. To the contrary, the constitutional prohibition against cruel and unusual punishment, like other provisions of the Bill of Rights, was designed expressly to protect the weak and powerless from the passions, or the reckless neglect, of the majority and its leaders. 443 F.Supp. at 979.

For each factual finding of a legitimate plaintiff grievance, the court methodically cited federal precedent to support the posture that each such condition alone was sufficient for court intervention. Thus, with a veritable avalanche of authority, Judge Pettine concluded with ease that:

the evidence is overwhelming that the totality of conditions of confinement in Maximum and Medium do not provide the "tolerable living environment", *Rhem* v. *Malcolm,* 371 F.Supp. 594, 627 (S.D.N.Y.), *aff'd,* 507 F.2d 333 (2d Cir. 1974), that the Eighth and Fourteenth Amendments require for state prison inmates. Compare *Williams* v. *Edwards,* 547 F.2d 1206, 1211 (5th Cir.

1974); *Holt* v. *Sarver*, 442 F.2d 304, 308 (8th Cir. 1971); *Mitchell* v. *Untreiner*, 421 F.Supp. 886, 896 (N.D.Fla. 1976); *Pugh* v. *Locke*, 406 F.Supp. at 329; *Hamilton* v. *Schiro*, 338 F.Supp. 1016, 1019 (E.D.La. 1970). 443 F.Supp. at 979.

Remedy Imposed by the Court (1977 Order)

The court ordered the closing of the maximum-security facility within one year of its order. All awaiting pretrial detainees were ordered to be removed from the maximum-security facility within three months and provided certain minimal facilities in which to live. The population of the maximum-security facility was ordered to be reduced within nine months in accordance with a reclassification process promulgated by the court.

Defendants were ordered to bring the ACI into compliance with minimum standards for its food service, sanitation, lighting, plumbing, and insect and rodent control within six months. The court ordered specific building improvements to ACI facilities to be accomplished within nine months: adequate heating and ventilation, improved plumbing and sanitation, and so forth.

An adequate health-care delivery system was ordered created within six months. An effective drug-abuse program was ordered created within three months. A master was ordered appointed within thirty days to monitor compliance with and implementation of the relief ordered.

Pertinent Proceedings Subsequent to 1977 Order

In October 1977, the court appointed a special master with instructions, inter alia, to monitor the defendants' compliance with the court's order, to report to the court on a monthly basis, to recommend hiring and firing of ACI personnel, to institute inmate grievance procedures, to hold hearings appropriate to carry out his mandate, and to issue a comprehensive report in eighteen months. The master was authorized to hire one staff consultant and one full-time clerk-stenographer, paid for by the state. The master's office space and supplies were to be provided by the defendants.

In November 1977, the *Providence Journal* reported that Governor Garrahy claimed Judge Pettine "has already overstepped his bounds a number of times" and that to have the judge removed from the case would require the defendants "to present a case that he has lost objectivity."

Judge Pettine revealed his awareness of the tensions inherent in the American federal system when, in December 1977, he wrote the Rhode Island special assistant attorney general:

I realize the problems involved in implementing my order; of course, there must be room for maneuvering to accomplish each of its objectives. In addition, I have always been sensitive to the budgetary aspects, and it may be that the extent of some of the planned improvements may have to be further modified. If and when we are confronted with such issues, the Court will be prepared, for good cause shown through an evidentiary hearing, to reconsider specific paragraphs of the order.

I do not believe I am being expansive in saying that this case is being watched nationally because it is the first time, to my knowledge, when the State Executive and Federal Judicial branches of government have attempted a team-like approach to reform a prison. We can establish a model that will be cited with approval in the many states with similar problems. I will do everything I can to encourage a harmonious effort. However, this does not mean we abdicate our responsibilities—it cannot mean that: Adherence to our respective sworn duties should be in no way disruptive in accomplishing the many reforms.

1986 Court Findings of Fact and of Law

In May 1986, Judge Pettine issued a lengthy opinion and order,[4] summarized as follows.

Findings of Fact

Overcrowding. With a rated or design capacity of 186, the medium-security facility was found to have an actual population of 224. When compared to the original rated capacity, the inmate population there had increased over 50 percent.

Holding only pretrial detainees, the Intake Services Center (ISC) had a design capacity of 168, but actual population had reached as high as 347 in late 1985. Inmates in ISC were found to be double-celled in seventy-one square feet up to twenty hours each day.

Programming and idleness. "Virtually the same conditions" were found to exist in 1986 with regard to availability of rehabilitative and vocational programs for prisoners and to the idleness of inmates as existed in 1977 at the ACI.

Food facilities. More than fifteen serious violations of health regulations were found at the center kitchen, which prepared food for the entire ACI. "A serious health-threatening condition was permitted to develop and fester."

Environmental health problems. Numerous fire hazards, as well as plumbing, electrical, and heating deficiencies, were found to exist at the ACI.

[4] 639 F.Supp. 244.

Medical and mental health services. Few essential medical services, such as testing for tuberculosis among inmates, were found to exist at the ACI. Furthermore, too few mental health staff were available to the large prisoner population.

Findings of Law

The unappealed 1977 order finding violations of the Eighth Amendment remained consistent with subsequent decisions of the United States Supreme Court and, therefore, remained the law of the case requiring the defendants' compliance.

EXHIBIT ONE. Population of the Rhode Island Adult Correctional Institutions, 1972–1983

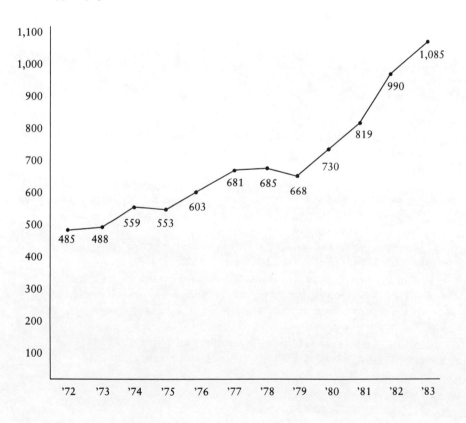

Appendix 2 *Keyes et al. v. School District No. 1*
United States Supreme Court; United States District Court, District of Colorado

Case history prepared by Kate Makuen

Summary

Keyes was the first case of northern, nonstatutory segregation in a public school system to come before the Supreme Court. While it did not eradicate the distinction between de jure and de facto segregation, it established that once the plaintiffs could prove even a circumscribed, localized area of de jure segregation, the burden of proof then shifted to the defendant to prove the absence of segregation. When the defendants failed to prove the absence of segregation, the school district, like their southern counterparts, had an affirmative duty to desegregate the schools. This was the first case in which the category "Hispanos" was used as a class in education discrimination.

The civil rights movement believed the court had widened the scope of inferences it was willing to make from limited factual findings. The court, however, in *Milliken v. Bradley,* 418 U.S. 717 (1974), later narrowed its interpretation.

The court-ordered integration plan for Denver has been both hailed as an exemplary model of citizen participation and monitoring and dismissed as yet another incrementalist and ineffectual attempt in achieving true equal opportunity in education.

APPENDIX 2

Introduction

Like most large cities, in the 1960s Denver underwent major demographic changes, whose impact was felt on housing patterns and public school enrollments. As the population of black and Hispanic people increased, so did the segregation of neighborhoods and schools.

School District No. 1 is coterminous with the city and county of Denver, covering an area of one hundred square miles. The overall racial and ethnic composition of the Denver public schools was 66 percent Anglo, 14 percent black, and 20 percent Hispano. In 1969 there were 119 schools with 96,580 pupils.

Major Parties

The original plaintiffs were composed of eight minority families, specifically, the parents of black and Mexican-American schoolchildren. (Only one family had a Hispanic surname.) They eventually filed a class action suit. Their attorneys were James Nabrit and Gordon Greiner. The case was supported by the National Association for the Advancement of Colored People Legal Defense and Education Fund (NAACP LDF).

The defendants were the school district; the board of education; the president, vice-president, and members of the board; the superintendent of schools; and several, presumably white, parents. Several amicus briefs were filed, by the U.S. Department of Justice, the National Education Association, the Colorado Education Association, and others.

Chronology

1968. The school board decided to adopt an integration plan that included busing.

1969. In school board election, two pro-busing candidates lost. Mandatory busing rescinded, replaced with a voluntary transfer system.

June 1969. Injunction sought in district court by eight minority (black and Mexican-American) parents of schoolchildren.

July 1969. District court granted application for a preliminary injunction. 303 F.Supp. 279.

August 1969. Court issues temporary restraining order and findings and opinion as to applicability of Section 407(a) of the Civil Rights Act of 1964. 303 F.Supp. 289.

December 1969. Court orders that plaintiffs may maintain this action as a class action.

March 1970. Court's third opinion, on merits, filed.

May 1970. District court ruled, in fourth opinion, on remedy, in partial favor to the plaintiffs. 313 F.Supp. 90.

June 1970. Respondent school board appealed, and petitioners cross-appealed, to the Court of Appeals for the Tenth Circuit.

October 1971. District court filed an unreported opinion, granting relief to two schools.

From 1969 to 1971, the Tenth Circuit Court of Appeals filed five unreported opinions: vacating preliminary injunctions, staying preliminary injunctions, ruling on motion to amend stay, denying motions to dismiss, and granting stay.

March 1971. Tenth Circuit Court of Appeals sustained part of district court's finding and reversed part of it.

February 1972. Supreme Court granted plaintiffs' petition for certiorari.

October 1972. Case argued before Supreme Court.

June 22, 1973. case decided. Judgment of court of appeals modified to vacate instead of reverse final decree. Cross-petition of school board denied. Case remanded to district court. 413 U.S. 189, 93 S.Ct. 2686.

December 1973. District court decides in favor of plaintiffs. 368 F.Supp. 207 (D.Colo. 1973).

April 8, 1974. Judge Doyle of district court orders school board to adopt Finger Plan by September. Plan requires school board to submit periodic and specific reports detailing their status of compliance with the decree. 380 F.Supp. 673 (D.Colo. 1974).

October 1974. Judge Doyle extends temporary restraining order prohibiting citizens' group from promoting boycotts to protect busing.

1975. Congress of Hispanic Educators attempts to appeal district court ruling to include bilingual education and other programs for specifically Hispanic, as opposed to minority, students. Circuit court denies, reaffirming the primacy of desegregation. Court affirms in part and reverses in part Judge Doyle's plan, remands back to district court with instruction to convert half-day plan into full-day plan. 521 F.2d. 465 (10th Cir. 1975). Supreme Court denies certiorari. 96 S.Ct. 806.

1975. Governor Lamm signs bill for $2.55 million bilingual-bicultural education program in Colorado.

1975. District court orders school board to alter their affirmative action plan so that it attains a better ratio of minority teachers, staff, and administrators.

1976. Supreme Court denies petitions for certiorari by school district and intervenors. 423 U.S. 1066 (1976).

1977. Plaintiffs and intervenors successfully sue for attorneys' fees and costs. District court awards these under Civil Rights Attorney's Fees Award Act and Emergency School Aid Act. 439 F.Supp. 393 (August 1977).

1977. District court orders the formation of a Community Education Council monitoring group.

1977. Hispanic Intervenors, Garcia et. al., seeking to stop the court-ordered desegregation in a neighborhood school, file class action suit to reopen the case in the circuit court.

1978. Circuit court decides not to reopen. 573 F.2d. 676.

July 1979. Newly appointed Judge Richard Matsch of district court orders school district to proceed with implementation of school closings and pupil assignments.

September 1980. District court orders school district to report to the court information regarding racial and ethnic composition of teachers with respect to their policies of hiring, promotion, and firing.

November 1980. Plaintiff-intervenor files a complaint using a claim under a provision of the Equal Educational Opportunity Act of 1974, regarding students who are limited-English proficient.

1981. School board proposes to district court a "freedom-of-choice" plan that would allow students in a variety of academic magnet schools to attend any schools to draw white students to minority neighborhoods.

November 1981. Judge Matsch orders defendants to file a "definitive plan for removal of racial discrimination in public education and for the establishment of a unitary school system."

May 1982. Judge Matsch rules that the school district's modified consensus desegregation plan would be accepted for a single school year, where it was an expedient in order to accommodate a move to middle schools and would attenuate the divisive effects of factionalism in the board. 540 F.Supp. 399.

1982. Data presented during court hearings shows that if students attended schools nearest to their homes under proposed board plan, the district would resegregate.

1983. Judge Matsch rules in favor of plaintiff-intervenors and holds that evidence supports certification of limited-English proficient children as a class and deficiencies in school system's transitional bilingual program warrants action to remedy equal educational opportunities for such students. 576 F.Supp. 1503.

January 1984. Board files in district court to have school district declared unitary. U.S. Justice Department files amicus curiae on the defendants' motions.

June 1985. Judge Matsch denies board's request. Board appeals to Tenth Circuit Court to keep options open, rather than reverse lower court ruling.

November 1985. Judge Matsch issues order for board to report back in 1986.

1986. Board submits status report to court.

1987. February: School district's proposal for three magnet school programs approved. Plaintiffs' alternative proposals and requests for further relief are denied.

March 1987. School district is still under court order. Plaintiffs have not submitted a complaint but have resubmitted the strict language of the 1974 order as the provisions of a modified final judgment. Defendants want the order to end. Attorneys will meet to declare which parts of original court order are valid and which should be vacated. They will construct an interim order to be in effect until November, at which time a pretrial conference will take place.

History before Litigation

In 1968 the Denver School Board by its own initiative decided to integrate 7 of the 119 schools by the implementation of busing. From the outset, this decision was controversial. The policy was embodied in Resolutions 1520, 1524, and 1531, by which the board desegregated the schools in the Park Hill area in the northeast portion of the city. Black expansion into the Park Hill area was dramatically visible, because the area historically had been insulated from the core city area by the six-lane Colorado Boulevard. When the barrier was breached, racism flourished. When the program was started, thirty-eight buses were damaged or destroyed. From that time until 1973, when the case appeared before the Supreme Court, the number of white pupils had dropped by over three thousand.

In the 1969 election, overturning the busing policy was the pivotal issue. When two antibusing candidates won, the newly constituted board replaced mandatory busing with a voluntary transfer system. In that election, Mexican-American parents voted antibusing by a ratio of 4 to 1, whereas black parents in a survey indicated by a ratio of two-thirds a preference for busing.

That Denver's integration issue ended up in federal court was as much a function of events inside the city as events outside it. More specifically, the case was shaped by the intervention of the NAACP Legal Defense and Education Fund. (The Mexican-American Legal Defense and Education Fund [MALDEF] did not enter the case until 1975.) The interest of the civil rights group stemmed from their need to get a precedent-setting case for two different reasons. The first reason was political: they needed the court to make the connection between some intentional government involvement in de jure segregation and systemic de jure or de facto segregation in the North. Efforts to invoke the Fourteenth Amendment without proving intent, while successful in some lower federal courts, failed in cases in large midwestern cities (Gary, Kansas City, Cincinnati). These defeats proved bitter and demoralizing for the NAACP LDF. Lower courts had already found de jure segregation in Detroit, Pontiac, Dayton, and Indianapolis. Cases similar to the Denver case were pending in Milwaukee, Boston, Kalamazoo, and Grand Rapids. Denver was selected because it seemed manageable and it had three elements at issue: a nullification, disputed findings of de jure discrimination, and a variant of de facto theory.

The political context under the Nixon administration is important to remember. The Justice Department's amicus brief did ask for more desegregation in the Park Hill area but supported integration for only part of the city and left a heavy burden of proof on the plaintiffs. Justice still supported the school-by-school approach. The Department of Health, Education, and Welfare Office for Civil Rights saw its enforcement of integration—the power to assure compliance or cut off funds for noncompliance with the Civil Rights Act of 1964—downgraded during the Nixon years.

The NAACP had pressing internal organizational concerns as well. They needed to reaffirm the value of their strategy of making school integration the highest priority for all of their state and local affiliates. In 1973 the Atlanta branch had moved toward accepting a compromise school integration plan that would have permitted a minimum of integration and busing of children in favor of more jobs, including the post of superintendent, for black people in the school system. Furthermore, the Atlanta NAACP president and the black school board members wanted the national organization to focus on cities with majority black school systems. In August 1973 the national group forced its strongest local unit back into line by giving it an ultimatum. A lack of cohesion and coordination would set back the fight, the national leaders said, and "the courts would begin to take notice of our change of position."[1]

The NAACP Legal Defense Fund's ability to raise money from predominantly white liberal individuals and foundations was premised on the virtue of school integration. Racial balancing was believed to be the answer to educational achievement for black children; if the civil rights movement lost on the issue of desegregation, a domino effect that would reverse gains made by black Americans might result.

The Decision to Litigate

The plaintiffs alleged that the school district, acting in its capacity as an agent of the state of Colorado, had violated constitutional rights of the minority schoolchildren. Plaintiffs first filed a request for an injunction against the "recission" of the resolutions taken in 1969 and an order directing the board to readopt the

[1]*New York Times* and Derrick A. Bell, Jr., "Serving Two Masters," 85 *Yale Law Journal* 470–516 (March 1976).

three resolutions in the Park Hill area. The school system had never been operated under a constitutional or statutory provision that mandated or permited racial segregation in public education.[2]

The plaintiffs alleged that decisions regarding school construction and attendance boundaries were made pursuant to a segregative policy, in violation of the principles enumerated in *Brown,* and that Denver schools showing high concentrations of minority students offered an inferior educational opportunity, in violation of the Fourteenth Amendment.

The district court found that by the construction of a new, relatively small elementary school, Barrett, in the middle of the black community west of Park Hill, by the gerrymandering of student attendance zones, by the use of so-called optional zones, and by the excessive use of mobile classroom units, among other things, the respondent school board, for over almost a decade after 1960, had engaged in an unconstitutional policy of deliberate racial segregation with respect to the Park Hill schools. The court ordered the board to desegregate the Park Hill schools only, through the implementation of the three rescinded resolutions. 303 F.Supp. 279 and 289 (1969).

Issues Attendant to Lower Court Litigation

Thus began the the lengthy course of litigation over school desegregation in Denver. Upon securing the initial order of the district court directing relief, the plaintiffs, recognizing that the desegregation of Park Hill was insufficient, expanded their suit to secure desegregation of *all* the remaining schools in the district, particularly the heavily segregated schools in the core city area. The district court denied further relief. The court concluded that its finding of a purposeful and systematic program of racial segregation in the Park Hill area did *not* impose on the school board an affirmative duty to eliminate segregation throughout the district. The court fractionated the district and held that plaintiffs had to make a fresh showing of de jure segregation in each area of the city for which they sought relief.

In a restrictive reasoning, the court held that its finding of segregative intent in one area was not material to the question of segregative intent in other areas of the city. The district court did, however, find that the core city schools were

[2]To the contrary, the Colorado Constitution, Article IX, Section 8, expressly prohibits any "classification of pupils . . . on account of race or color." As early as 1927, the Colorado Supreme Court held that a Denver practice of excluding black students from school programs at Manual High School and Morey Junior High School violated state law. *Jones* v. *Newlong,* 81 Color. 25, 253 P 386.

educationally inferior to the predominantly "Anglo" schools. It ruled that the board must provide compensatory education in "substantially equal facilities."[3]

The district court was faced with the issue of determining whether or not official segregation within a school district blemished the entire district with respect to its racial balance. That court, like other lower federal courts, simply lacked guidance from the Supreme Court at that time. Working in an area of largely unfashioned law, the lower courts tried to be innovative.

The school board appealed, and the plaintiffs cross-appealed. On appeal, Judge Hill for the Tenth Circuit Court affirmed the Park Hill ruling and agreed that the deliberate segregation found there proved nothing regarding an overall policy of segregation. The court reversed the legal determination of the district court that the core city schools were educationally inferior and thus set aside the part of the final decree pertaining to compensatory education. 445 F.2d. 990 (1971). The plaintiffs appealed to the Supreme Court.

The Supreme Court Decision

Upon appeal from the plaintiffs, the Supreme Court handed down an 8–1 ruling. The Court reviewed the decision as to the core city schools and ruled on five issues. First, it modified the court of appeals' judgment to vacate instead of reverse the district court's decree. Second, it remanded the case to the district court. The lower court was to (1) allow the school board an opportunity to prove that the Park Hill area should be treated as isolated from the rest of the district; (2) should the school board fail to prove that contention, reach a determination of whether the Denver school system is a dual school system by reason of the Park Hill segregation, which would require desegregation of the entire school system "root and branch"; and (3) if the Denver school system were not a dual school system by reason of the Park Hill desegregation, allow the school board an opportunity to rebut the prima facie case of intentional segregation in the core city schools made by the finding of intentional segregation in the Park Hill schools. The defendants had to come forward with exculpatory evidence to prove that there would have been segregation without their misconduct.

[3]313 F.Supp. 90, 96 (1970). One observer noted that the court was using "separate but equal" doctrine, from *Plessy*, to justify desegregation policy that should have been derived, legally, from *Brown*. Robert L. Herbst, "The Legal Struggle to Integrate Schools in the North," 407 *The Annals* 43–60 (1973).

The Court found that proof of intentional localized segregation in neighborhood schools had probative value, and warranted a citywide remedy.[4]

The Supreme Court's ruling, while a victory for the civil rights movement, was a mixed blessing. The NAACP LDF had hoped that the Court would reverse its traditional insistence that intent had to be shown by the plaintiffs in desegregation cases. The failure to convince the Court to invalidate the remedial immunity of de facto desegregation meant that future plaintiffs would still have to prove intentional segregation in a "meaningful or significant" portion of a school system, before the burden of proof would shift to the defendants. Litigation would continue to be difficult and expensive.[5] Justices Douglas and Powell concurred with the majority opinion but dissented in part, urging the court to invalidate the distinction between de jure and de facto.

The Court extended its requirements of southern school systems to those of the North, where statutory dual systems never existed, but where school authorities carried out a systematic program of segregation. The reasoning was grounded in *Green v. County School Board*, 391 U.S. 430 (1968), where the Virginia State school board had an "affirmative duty . . . to convert to a unitary system." In *Swann v. Charlotte-Mecklenberg Board of Education*, 402 U.S. 1 (1971) the Court held in a North Carolina case that the question is not what percentage of causation stems from "discriminatory action by school authorities" but, rather, whether the necessary remedial action is within the power or "jurisdiction" of school (even if conditions stem from residential patterns). In *Keyes* the *Green* duty was rendered as a judicially ordered exercise of the initial affirmative jurisdictional powers.

Enforcement and Postdecision Litigation of Remedial Plan

Policy, of course, is not equivalent to an official act of law. There remained a complex process of working out the implementation of the district court's order on remand. Eventually, the district court ordered the school board to

---

[4]Another district court had reached the same conclusions that the Denver court had, holding that the mere fact that the employment of a neighborhood school policy served to perpetuate existing racial balance did not render such a policy violative of equal protection. *Gomperts v. Chase* 329 F.Supp. 1192 (N.D.Cal. 1971). 9 *New England Law Review* 341–57 (1974). After *Keyes*, courts no longer required proof of citywide constitutional violations in order for the remedy of citywide busing to be enacted.

[5]"Public School Segregation and the Contours of Unconstitutionality: The Denver School Board Case," 45 *University of Colorado Law Review* 457–85 (1974), and Herbst, "Legal Struggle," 43.

adopt the Finger Plan, conceived by consultant Dr. John Finger, among several competing alternatives. 368 F.Supp. 207 (D. Colo. 1973) and 380 F.Supp. 673 (D.Colo. 1974). That the plan was not adopted without struggle is evident by reviewing the list of intervenors, many of whom had their own views and alternative plans: Mexican American Legal Defense Fund, Congress of Hispanic Educators, Montbello Citizens' Committee, Inc., Moore School Community Association and Moore School Lay Advisory Committee, Legal Aid Society of Metropolitan Denver, North Denver Legal Services, Eastside Legal Services for United Parents of Northeast Denver, Citizens Association for Neighborhood Schools, and Concerned Citizens for Quality Education.

The school district's plan, entitled "A Plan for Expanding Educational Opportunity in the Denver Public Schools," was rejected as unconstitutional and equitably defective because its definition of a desegregated school as one having an enrollment of 25 to 75 percent Anglo students was inadequate. It failed to achieve integration, and it involved closing structurally sound intercity schools, which would inevitably result in changing the character of areas favorably located for achieving integrated neighborhoods and schools.

The plaintiffs' plan, entitled "Proposals for District-Wide Desegregation and Quality Education," was also rejected because, although it met constitutional standards for desegregating a dual system, it achieved that goal at the expense of excessive busing.

The so-called Cardenas Plan, which recommended making the system more compatible to the minority child's economic orientations and his or her cultural and language orientation, was not adopted for the entire district. During the evidentiary hearings much of the opposition to the plan concerned the practicality of the plan and problems of its implementation rather than the educational principles espoused. Judge Doyle, however, approved the use of the Cardenas Plan as a "pilot program" in three predominantly Hispanic schools, which would remain segregated.

The Finger Plan involved rezoning of twenty-four schools, pairing (by classroom or home school) of thirty-three schools, the assignment of students from satellite areas (one-way busing), and reassignment. Programs such as instruction of students in race relations, support groups for parents and teachers, transportation, and affirmitive action hiring were ordered. Part of Judge Doyle's plan was half-day integration of all but a few schools. The court of appeals later ordered full-day integration of all schools in the city. 521 F.2d 465 (10th Cir. 1975).

The district court initially ordered the school board to make periodic and specific reports to the court on the status of the implementation. Later, in 1977, the court assigned the task of monitoring to a committee, the Community Education Council. The Denver CEC, in contrast to monitoring committees in other cities, was organized around complaint resolution, not systemwide research and analysis. Several hundred residents were trained and deployed by the monitoring body to go into the schools and report back to the CEC. The CEC was given authority to review all school district proposals which would have an impact on the desegregation effort, and it had access to and influence in the courts. It persuaded the court, for example, to order activity buses for children who wanted to participate in extracurricular activities.

While widely hailed as a success, there is some disagreement about the actual effectiveness of the CEC. According to one account, the Denver CEC has been one of the most successful and influential of its kind in the country.[6] Another account argues that while citizen monitoring fosters a sense of popular control, in general it has a minimal effect on legal compliance or policy implementation.[7] The CEC was disbanded in 1984.

With respect to the role of the school board, the extremely adversarial atmosphere that prevailed around the case initially has become more harmonious. The new school superintendent, who began in 1985, is proud of the achievements of the school system. In 1986 the board passed Resolution 2233, a statement of its intent to maintain an integrated system. A board-level committee is working with the superintendent to produce a comprehensive annual report to the court. In Barrett School, one site of the original litigation, the enrollment of Anglo students is up to 30 percent of the school population. A program of "affirmative student placement" tries to locate students in order to ameliorate disproportionate racial assignments in general, rather than absolute, ratios.

It is not clear if any group presently has the responsibility of monitoring the enforcement of school integration in Denver. While the plaintiffs have not filed a complaint, they have been resistant to changing the strict language of the 1974 order in current negotiations with the board regarding the wording of an interim order.

Monitoring the court order had never been the concern of the attorneys. James Nabrit, counsel for the plaintiffs and former second-ranking officer of the LDF at the time, saw the fund as having a law-making, rather than an enforcement, role.[8] Yet given the amount and intensity of litigation since the order was implemented, it seemed that even a relatively small city such as

---

[6]Willis D. Hawley et al., *Strategies for Effective School Desegregation* (Lexington, Mass.: Lexington Books, 1983). The authors interviewed eight people in Denver and based their conclusions on these interviews.

[7]Jennifer Hochschild, *The New American Dilemma* (New Haven: Yale University Press, 1984), p. 112.

[8]Gary Orfield, *Must We Bus?* (Washington, D.C.: Brookings Institution, 1978).

Denver was unmanageable. After the Detroit case of *Milliken*, the LDF was pessimistic about finding plans for large cities. In the four years after *Keyes* the LDF filed no new northern school case in any city bigger than Springfield, Illinois.

The role of the Hispanic plaintiff-intervenors relates to the inclusion of diverse parties in a class action suit. The specific needs of Hispanic children, as differentiated from black children, were not at issue in the initial litigation of *Keyes*. Following *Brown*, the question of classification of Mexican-Americans for school desegregation was still unresolved. In *Romero v. Weakley* (1955), settled out of court, blacks and Hispanics challenged the practice of classifying Hispanics as "whites" and mixing them into black schools for purposes of desegregation. In *Hernandez v. Driscoll Consolidated School District* (1957) a court ruled that it was unconstitutional for the district to assign Hispanic students to language classes on the basis of "race" rather than lack of English-language skills. Also, the court identified Hispanos as being subject to "unreasonable race discrimination." In 1970, in *Cisneros v. Corpus Christi Independent School District*, 467 F2d. 142 (5th Cir. 1972), a Texas court held that Mexican-Americans constituted an identifiable class for purposes of the Fourteenth Amendment. Not until *Keyes* however, did the Court recognize Hispanics in the Southwest as being discriminated against and segregated in a manner similar to blacks.

Guidelines for sound educational policy remain unclear. When desegregation and bilingual education compete with one another, the courts have found the latter is not a substitute for the former. In Denver, MALDEF tried to explain to an unsympathetic Hispanic community that desegregation was inevitable and that it could be a vehicle for improving education for their children. The district court had, after all, left a few Hispano schools segregated so that their administrators could conduct experiments in bilingual-bicultural education. The school board opposed judicial intervention, and when the Community Education Council monitoring group charged that the board was sabotaging bilingual education, the board appealed to the circuit court. In August 1975, the circuit court sustained the board's challenge and reversed the requirements for bilingual education, ruling that the predominantly Hispanic schools be desegregated. 521 F.2d at 482. In Colorado presently, some bilingual instruction continues in some schools; it is funded with state money. English as a Second Language is taught at the high school level.

Left unresolved were the status of Hispanic schoolchildren outside the Southwest and the status of other limited-English-proficient groups, such as Native Americans and Indochinese refugees. In a 1974 case involving Chinese students in San Francisco, the Court rejected the assumption that it is the responsibility of immigrant children to learn English on their own. *Lau v.*

Nichols, 414 U.S. 563 (1974). The *Lau* decision was seen to compete with *Keyes,* in that it proposed group solidarity, rather than inclusion, as a remedy. MALDEF jettisoned its support of desegregation, leaving that task to the NAACP LDF, and joined the Legal Services lawyers and the Puerto Rican Legal Defense and Education Fund in supporting bilingual programs.

Conclusions

Judicial intervention in public schools to promote equal educational opportunity by achieving racial balance has been eclipsed in recent years by other issues, such as special education, the drug problem, and the First, Fourth, and Fifth Amendment rights of students. School boards are sued often on a variety of issues. Yet fourteen years after the *Keyes* decision and the implementation of the remedial plan, the defendants and the plaintiffs still disagree about whether the public schools have provided significantly better education for minority, especially lower-income minority, children. This question, of course, is a national problem. As one writer commented, some of the district courts saw a right to equal educational opportunity as quite distinct from the right to nonsegregated education. The Supreme Court, however, finding the existence of dual systems, did not develop a "less-onerous alternative" of equal educational opportunity. To expect the schools to deal with disparities stemming from historical factors largely beyond their control is a tall order.[9]

The issue of judicial intervention into public schools relates to the evolution of urban politics. Many large cities now have a majority of minority students in their school systems, due to "white flight" to the suburbs as well as the lack of incentives to encourage individuals from either race to move into opposite-race communities. In Denver, white flight from black schools has been three times that from Hispanic schools, because while educational levels of Hispanics are lower, their income levels are higher. The costs of white flight are considerable. The Supreme Court, however, in keeping with its concern about disguised discrimination, forbade lower federal courts and school authorities from allowing the possibility of white flight to affect their school desegregation efforts. *U.S. v. Scotland Neck Board of Education,* 407 U.S. 484 (1972). The policy options discussed assume it is desirable and worth the expense to retain whites in desegregating school systems and to impose a disproportionate share of the burden of busing on minority children. That assumption is very troublesome to some nonwhite parents.

Many cities, having experienced inflation, tax limitation movements, ero-

[9]Peter B. Kutner, "Keyes v. School District Number One: A Constitutional Right to Equal Educational Opportunity?" 8 *Journal of Law and Education* 1–43 (1979).

sion of the tax base, and cuts in state and federal aid, are under fiscal strain. Political support for public education and white as well as black support for integration have all waned. It will be interesting to see the impact, if any, of increased black electoral power in urban areas on the future of city schools.

Appendix 3 *Perez et al.* v. *Boston Housing Authority* Suffolk Superior Court, Suffolk County, Massachusetts

Case history prepared by Jane Fountain

Summary

In 1975 nine tenants of Boston public housing, representing all Boston Housing Authority (BHA) tenants, filed a complaint in the Housing Court for the City of Boston charging the BHA with widespread violations of the state sanitary code. The court ruled in their favor; however, the court's orders have yet to be fully implemented.

The court originally issued orders to the BHA, which was unable and unwilling to carry them out. A master was appointed, first to offer expert assistance to the BHA, then, increasingly, to control the management and operations of the authority. When this remedy failed, the parties entered into protracted negotiations, the outcome of which was a consent decree to which the parties agreed to be bound. Under the consent decree the condition of many public housing units actually deteriorated, and vacancy rates increased. The consent decree was vacated, and the BHA was put into receivership in 1980.

The receivership has entered a restorative phase, with partial control of the BHA returned to the city of Boston. Although substantial progress has been made toward compliance with the state sanitary code, as of the spring of 1987 the court continues to monitor the BHA's progress.

Chronology

1967. Citizens' Housing and Planning Association study of the BHA cites major problems in many of Boston's public housing developments.

1970. Several tenants of the BHA's D Street development file suit in superior court seeking to have the BHA and the Department of Community Affairs (the DCA) maintain the development in compliance with the state sanitary code. Superior court dismisses the suit. The Supreme Judicial Court affirms the dismissal.

1972. HUD conducts a comprehensive management review of the BHA. It documents substantial deficiencies in BHA's operations.

1973. Citizens' Housing and Planning Association study of the BHA, 1969–73, makes findings similar to its 1967 study.

1974. Tenants of the BHA file suit in U.S. District Court. The suit is dismissed.

*February 7, 1975. Perez et al. v. *Boston Housing Authority:* initiation of litigation.[1] Original litigation also joins "State defendants," notably, the secretary of communities and development, the commissioner of the DCA, and the treasurer and governor of Massachusetts.

*March 28, 1975, ff. The Boston Housing Court rules that the BHA is liable and the DCA is legally required to fund efforts to rectify sanitary code violations which the BHA is unable to fund. The DCA appeals the ruling to the State Superior Court.

*March–April 1975. The housing court issues several interim orders to the BHA to remedy "especially intolerable conditions." The court orders the BHA to hold a conference with the parties and interested tenants to consider mechanisms for community involvement in devising rehabilitation plans. The consensus of conference participants is that the BHA requires expert assistance to accomplish any improvements. The tenants present a draft order for appointment of a receiver; BHA files a draft order regarding appointment of a master.

*May 22, 1975. The court rejects the appointment of a receiver. Robert B. Whittlesey is appointed as master chiefly to prepare plans for the maintenance and rehabilitation of the properties. The BHA is ordered to assist the master.

*July 10, 1975. The Supreme Judicial Court reverses the lower court's decision requiring the DCA to fund efforts at ameliorization and dismisses the state defendants from the action but remands the case to the housing court for further proceedings.

*May 22, 1975–September 1, 1976. Twenty-five interim orders are issued by

---

[1]Major court proceedings are preceded by an asterisk.

the court primarily to require limited but immediate improvements. At hearings held with regard to BHA's implementation of interim orders, the court finds several failures to carry out its orders.

July 1, 1976. The master files with the court a five-volume report critical of the BHA and its board and containing specific and detailed recommendations for procedural and substantive changes. The board moves to strike the report and seeks the termination of the master's and the court's involvement in the case.

August 4, 1976, ff. The plaintiffs file a motion seeking the appointment of a receiver for the BHA. A hearing on the motion is scheduled for September 3, 1976. Hearing is postponed after the parties and the Tenants' Policy Council agree to attempt to negotiate. The court participates in several hundred hours of negotiations at the request of the parties.

October 6, 1976. Judge Paul Garrity retires from the housing court and accepts appointment as a judge of the superior court. The case is transferred to the superior court in order for it to remain in the same judicial hands.

June 1, 1977. A consent decree, the joint product of negotiations, takes effect. The master is charged with monitoring progress and compliance of the BHA.

September 1977. Samuel Thompson, administrator of the BHA, resigns effective October 17, 1977. The board appoints Kevin Feeley to be acting administrator for ninety days.

January 11, 1978. The board votes to extend the appointment of Acting Director Feeley for an indefinite period.

March 13, 1978. The court orders the board to appoint a permanent administrator. Bradley Biggs is appointed.

November 1978. After twenty-nine formal modifications of the consent decree, most extending time for various BHA submissions, the master forwards to the BHA approximately twenty-six notices of substantial noncompliance.

December 28, 1978, ff. The tenants charge the BHA with pervasive failure to meet the demands of the decree. They request that the consent decree be vacated and that a receiver be appointed. The BHA files responses. The court consolidates the applications for hearing.

March 26–May 23, 1979. The case is heard.

July 2, 1979. The BHA Board authorizes its chairperson to extend all employment agreements with senior management employees for a period of two years (to "boost morale").

July 25, 1979. Judge Garrity orders (1) a recertification of the plaintiff class to include all residential tenants of BHA properties in which exist present or future violations of the state sanitary code, (2) immediate vacation of the consent decree, (3) appointment of a receiver whose powers shall totally supersede those of the board, (4) appointment of an advisory committee to advise the receiver and the court, and (5) several interim orders to prevent further regression of BHA operations until the receiver takes office.

February 4, 1980. On appeal from the BHA, the Supreme Judicial Court affirms the judgment of the superior court to place BHA in temporary receivership.

February 5, 1980. Superior court orders the appointment of Lewis H. (Harry) Spence as receiver and discharges Robert B. Whittlesey, the master, effective February 29, 1980.

February 7, 1980. Superior court orders the appointment of the Housing Advisory Committee.

February 18, 1983. Judge Garrity orders court receivership of the BHA to continue for another year.

October 1983. Collective bargaining agreement made between the BHA and its 350 craft workers. Twenty generic semiskilled maintenance worker positions created. Craft workers agree to relax jurisdictional lines between some jobs so that about thirty maintenance tasks can be performed by any craft worker. In exchange, BHA makes considerable financial concessions to workers.

January 1984. Mayor Kevin White steps down. Raymond Flynn takes office as mayor of Boston. Garrity says receivership may be lifted in late summer if plans can be made to preserve gains that have been made under receivership. Garrity and Spence cite election of Flynn and rewriting of BHA's collective bargaining agreement with its 350 craft workers as key developments.

February 1984. Tenants request extension of receivership for another year. Garrity extends court's control of BHA for a year.

October 18, 1984. Superior court transfers full authority of the BHA from the receiver to the mayor of Boston to remain in effect until October 18, 1986 (subsequently extended until January 5, 1987). Restorative phase of the action begins.

August 10, 1984. Harry Spence leaves position as receiver of the BHA.

January 7, 1987. Superior court (per Justice Harry Elam) orders the mayor to continue to exercise the powers formerly vested in the receiver through December 31, 1987.

Prelitigation History

Introduction

Before 1980, the BHA functioned as a semiautonomous body with a five-member board of commissioners responsible for policy-making and long-range planning and an administrator responsible for management and operations. The mayor of Boston appointed four of the board members (with approval of the city council); the governor appointed the fifth member.

When the litigation began, the BHA owned and operated nineteen federally aided developments for low-income families comprising a total of 10,348 dwelling units (73 percent of such units in the commonwealth), ten state-aided developments for low-income families (3,681 units, 27 percent of such units in the commonwealth), 25 federally aided developments for the low-income elderly (2,613 units, 94 percent of such units in the commonwealth), and two state-aided developments for elderly persons of low income (160 units, 60 percent of such units in the commonwealth). The BHA leased 2,655 dwelling units from private landlords in accord with various federal programs (97 percent of such units in the commonwealth), and 59 units under various state programs (3 percent of such units in the commonwealth). Approximately 55,000 people, more than 10 percent of the total population of Boston, live in BHA-owned and -leased housing.[2]

Since the sixties, criticism of the BHA's management and operation of its public housing developments has been a commonplace. For example, a 1967 study concluded: "The quality of maintenance in most projects is far below acceptable standards. . . . Most Housing Authority positions are regarded as being in the patronage category, to be filled by directive from City Hall. . . . The system leads to poor work performance and inadequate supervisory mechanisms."[3] Moreover, management reviews conducted in the 1970s by the United States Department of Housing and Urban Development found serious deficiencies. The 1972 review criticized the BHA for delays in the repair of vacated apartments, which led to vandalism and rental losses; severe problems in financial planning, reporting and control with budgets that were consistently late and of little value; lack of performance appraisals for personnel; and political considerations in supervision and disciplinary actions. The 1976 management review was even more critical of the BHA, finding that financial management in any meaningful sense was nonexistent.[4]

In 1973 a privately sponsored study of the BHA cited maintenance as one of the BHA's most critical problems. It also criticized the lifetime tenure system

---

[2]Perez v. Boston Housing Authority, 368 Mass. 333, 342 (1975).

[3]Citizens' Housing and Planning Association, *Public Housing at the Crossroads: The Boston Housing Authority* (1967).

[4]United States Department of Housing and Urban Development, "Comprehensive Consolidated Management Review Report" (1972); "Management Review of the Boston Housing Authority" (1976).

(after five years of employment), political sponsorship of employees, and deficient management systems.[5]

Early Attempts at Litigation

Several tenants residing at the BHA's D Street development filed suit in superior court in 1970 seeking to have the BHA and the Massachusetts Department of Community Affairs (the DCA) maintain the development in compliance with the state sanitary code, the law that prescribes minimum fitness standards for human habitation. The suit was dismissed by the superior court. Dismissal was upheld by the Supreme Judicial Court, which ruled:

The case . . . resembles those more commonplace situations in which courts have regularly resisted the temptation to substitute their initiative or judgment for that of agencies charged . . . with primary responsibility for discretionary choices. . . . Courts, however, have been keen to override traditional limitations . . . when health or life was at stake. . . . So we might be impelled to require the Superior Court to accept the [suit] . . . if we were not persuaded that more effective . . . procedures are available for striving to achieve satisfactory conditions at this and other housing developments.[6]

Tenants of the BHA brought suit again in October 1974, this time in U.S. District Court. In dismissing the suit, the judge noted that the projects were in "a deplorable state of repair" but ruled that "the federal courts cannot pretend to be the cure-all for America's housing ills. Federal courts lack the expertise, the staff, and the Congressional mandate to do the job. . . . [T]he Housing Court for the City of Boston . . . is better suited to solve the enormous housing problems encountered by the tenants of Boston. Yet in the last analysis, long range answers can best be provided by the 'political branches' of government."[7] In addition to these cases, scores of complaints against the BHA were filed by its tenants in the Boston Housing Court. The complaints were corroborated by evidence that many public housing units and buildings were indecent, unsafe, and in violation of the state sanitary code.

[5]Citizens' Housing and Planning Association, *A Struggle for Survival: The Boston Housing Authority, 1969–73* (1973).

[6]*West Broadway Task Force, Inc. et al.* v. *Commissioner of the Department of Community Affairs et al.*, 363 Mass. 745, 751–52 (1973).

[7]*Boston Public Housing Tenants' Policy Council, Inc.* v. *Lynn*, 388 F.Supp. 493, 498 (D.Mass. 1974).

The Litigation

Perez et al. v. Boston Housing Authority (February 7, 1975)

As representatives of all BHA tenants, Armando Perez and eight other residents of several BHA developments filed a complaint in the Boston Housing Court against the BHA and other state defendants. They sought remedies for widespread violations of the state sanitary code in apartments and common areas of BHA's developments. Since it was widely known that the BHA had insufficient funds to make the needed repairs, they also sought to require the DCA to fund efforts at ameliorization. On March 28, 1975, the court ruled in the tenants' favor and found "countless violations of the State Sanitary Code . . . [which] result from vandalism and from BHA's inability to conduct routine maintenance at its developments and to replace antiquated heating, plumbing, electrical and other systems. . . . [T]he physical conditions existing in some, perhaps in many of BHA's apartments are so intolerable that relocation is immediately required."[8] The court also ruled that the DCA was legally required to fund efforts to rectify sanitary code violations which the BHA was financially unable to remedy.

In July 1975, the Supreme Judicial Court reversed the March 28 judgment on appeal from the DCA. But it remanded the case to the housing court. Although the Supreme Judicial Court thought there was room there for significant remedial action, it also acknowledged that its reversal rendered certain lower court orders impossible. Although the court could articulate the dilemma, it could not solve it. "The Commonwealth cannot be required to expend funds for rehabilitation of BHA property; yet hundreds, and probably thousands, of tenants are living in substandard units which the judge has characterized as 'not decent.' Without adequate funding, the alternatives appear equally unacceptable: either the tenants continue to live in conditions which are unlawful under the Sanitary Code, or the substandard units are to be withdrawn from use, with the accompanying probability of many persons left homeless."[9]

During the interim period between the housing court decision and the decision of the superior court (March to July 1975), Judge Garrity issued several interim orders in response to especially intolerable conditions in Boston's public housing developments. The orders to the BHA included the following: (1) develop criteria for identification of occupied apartments where conditions jeopardize the health, welfare, or safety of the tenants; (2) prepare a program for prompt inspection of every occupied apartment to identify apart-

---

[8]*Armando Perez et al. v. Boston Housing Authority,* "Findings, Rulings, Opinion, and Orders," March 28, 1975.

[9]*Perez et al. v. Boston Housing Authority,* 368 Mass. 333 (1975), pp. 341–42.

ments where such conditions exist; (3) prepare an evacuation plan for affected tenants or rectify such conditions immediately; (4) prepare responses to interim orders in consultation with tenants and appropriate agencies. In addition the court ordered the BHA to hold a conference to discuss mechanisms for using community resources for the rehabilitation of BHA's developments.

Appointment of the Master (May 22, 1975)

The BHA began filing written responses to the court's orders on April 11, 1975. The court found them inadequate. A consensus began to develop among the parties that the BHA required expert assistance to formulate the plans. The court requested the tenants and the BHA to discuss the possible appointment of a master or receiver to assist the BHA in carrying out the court's interim orders. The tenants filed an application with the court for the appointment of a receiver; the BHA filed a draft order for appointment of a master. At that time Judge Garrity rejected the more intrusive course of receivership. Instead, the court appointed Robert B. Whittlesey as master not only to provide expert assistance in responding to the interim orders but more important to prepare a comprehensive long-range plan and to draft interim orders as needed to remedy the violations of the state sanitary code in the BHA's developments. The BHA was ordered to assist the master and to furnish him with all required information.

Twenty-five interim orders, primarily for limited but immediate improvements, were issued to the BHA between May 22, 1975, and September 1, 1976. Hearings in connection with the BHA's implementation of these orders led Judge Garrity to conclude that there was a complete lack of coordination in the upper levels of the BHA staff. For example, the BHA was unable to replace roofing at its Mission Hill development, to submit budgets on time or in appropriate detail, and to supply a list of inadequate apartments at its Columbia Point and Mission Hill developments (which failure led to a contempt adjudication). Over time Judge Garrity became more critical of the BHA. "[The BHA] failed to comply with the Orders dated and made October 23, 1975 in this case for the reasons that BHA's Administrator, Assistant Administrator for Operations, General Counsel and Director of Maintenance, by their misfeasance and nonfeasance guaranteed that BHA would not comply with the Orders. The actions and inactions of those highest-level officials of BHA constitute severe mismanagement and that mismanagement is the principal reason why BHA did not comply with the . . . Orders."[10]

[10]*Perez,* "Findings, Rulings, and Orders," August 25, 1976.

On July 1, 1976, Robert Whittlesey filed a report on the BHA, as he had been ordered to do. The five-volume document noted that the BHA was near bankruptcy. It criticized maintenance operations as "an impenetrable morass" and modernization efforts as "grossly inefficient and slow." It cited security as a serious problem, due in part to a lack of monitoring of the security department. Tenant selection procedures were faulted for their lack of responsiveness to the problem of segregated housing and because staff failed to follow the plans that did exist, processing applications on an ad hoc basis. The report also criticized the lack of opportunity for tenant participation in the operations and rehabilitation of the developments. With regard to the internal administration of the BHA, the report found a tradition of employment on the basis of "political sponsorship and nepotism." It found "major problems in the capability of the BHA to communicate, implement and administer major policy decisions and programs." It found "little evidence that the Board is fully aware of the scope and seriousness of these problems or has provided the leadership necessary to resolve these major problems." As ordered, Whittlesey also set out detailed recommendations by issue area to address the problems reported.

In response, the Board of the BHA retained outside counsel, sought to strike the report from the court's records and to terminate the involvement of Robert Whittlesey and Judge Garrity in the case. To counter, the tenants again filed for the appointment of a receiver for the BHA. Afer a hearing to resolve these motions had been scheduled for mid-September 1976, the parties agreed to attempt to negotiate a settlement. The Boston Public Housing Tenants' Policy Council, Inc. joined in these negotiations.[11] At the request of the parties, the court also participated in what became several hundred hours of negotiations. During the negotiations, on October 6, 1976, Judge Garrity retired from the housing court to accept appointment as a judge of the superior court. (The *Perez* case was transferred to superior court so that it would remain in the same judicial hands.) The negotiations resulted in a lengthy and highly detailed consent decree which took effect on June 1, 1977, and to which the Board of the BHA agreed to be bound.

The Consent Decree

From the perspective of Judge Garrity the consent decree was best viewed as "an effort to achieve implementation of the recommendations set out in the

---

[11]In September 1975, the Tenants' Policy Council (the TPC) was allowed by the court to intervene in the case as an intervenor plaintiff broadly representative of the residents of BHA housing.

master's July 1, 1976, Report by means short of receivership." The decree consisted of three main sections. The first recertified the plaintiffs as a class, reappointed the master, and ordered periodic progress reports to be submitted to the court by the BHA and the master. The second specified procedural rules controlling the rights and responsibilities of the master, the BHA, the tenants and the Tenants' Policy Council. The third section delineated the specific goals of the decree and the framework by which the BHA was to achieve them in terms of thirteen plans in the following categories: Central Administration, Personnel, Finance, Purchasing, Central Stores, Maintenance, Data Processing, Management, Modernization, Security, Tenant Selection and Marketing, Evictions, and Legal. The thirteen plans varied as to specificity. In some cases the BHA was given specific directions; in others it was to develop "subplans" within certain guidelines and by given deadlines. The plans were designed with the BHA's budgetary constraints in mind so that improvements would not be delayed while the BHA searched for funding.

The master was given strong powers with respect to hiring and promotion at higher levels of the BHA. He was to assist the BHA in carrying out the provisions of the decree and was to monitor and report to the court on BHA performance. Any action that was seriously inconsistent with the decree would be considered substantial noncompliance. In such cases any party could give notice and, failing a mutually agreed-upon adjustment, could invoke a disputes procedure involving a court hearing and decision. The stated life of the consent decree was three years, but it could be vacated "at any time upon the application of any Party, if such Party demonstrates that, because of a change of law or any other reason, its further functioning will in all likelihood be so substantially unworkable that it will not substantially achieve the significant particular purposes of the Plans." Persistent failure to perform in good faith or willful and persistent interference were specifically mentioned as grounds for vacation of the decree.[12]

In November 1978, after one and a half years under the consent degree, the master sent some twenty-six notices of substantial noncompliance to the BHA. Twenty-nine formal modifications of the decree had been made previously, most extending deadlines for various submissions. Further requests by the BHA for extensions of deadlines were met with reluctance by the master and the Tenants' Policy Council as jeopardizing the time period agreed upon for the consent decree. The notices of noncompliance formed the basis of an application by the tenants under the disputes procedure. On the same day, December 28, 1978, the tenants also applied for vacation of the decree and temporary appointment of a receiver.

[12]N.B.: The BHA did not concede jurisdiction to the court to appoint a receiver.

The BHA's Performance under the Consent Decree

The tenants charged a pervasive failure of the BHA to meet the demands of the consent decree or to make any substantial progress toward improving the condition of substandard dwellings. The plaintiffs pointed to major failures of compliance related to the notices of substantial noncompliance in areas including security, repair or securing of vacant apartments, rerental of such units, consolidated budgets, financial forecasts and programs, central stores, work order procedure, and maintenance reorganization. The tenants also referred to obstructive interferences by board members in the day-to-day operations of the developments and criticized the board's selection and appointment of high-level BHA officials. The BHA filed responses to the tenants' charges. The court heard the case on thirty-five days, from March 26 to May 23, 1979.

Performance of the board. At the time of the hearing on the vacation of the consent decree, only four of the five seats on the BHA Board were filled. Three board members were asked to testify. (One board member had been appointed in January 1979 and therefore was not asked to testify.) Chairperson Barbara Carpenter, a former resident of Boston public housing, testified that she could remember no policy decisions made by the board during the past year. She testified to spending most of her time at the BHA "signing contracts, checks, and individual leases with the Authority's leased housing applicants." Otto Snowden, whose background is in community organizing, reported that he and his secretaries spent most of their time responding to tenants' complaints and requests. He testified that he tried to improve the BHA's image by relating to influential people how the master had sabotaged the BHA. He was unaware of the substance of any of the notices of substantial noncompliance, was unfamiliar with the BHA's fiscal situation, and was unaware that the vacancy rate in BHA developments had increased drastically during his tenure. John Battos, a former Massachusetts Bay Transit Authority vehicle operator and receipt receiver, knew nothing about the BHA's financial structure and operations except that it obtains money from HUD, the DCA, and rents. The court found that he had no real understanding of the provisions of the decree or of the BHA's performance under it. Overall, board members demonstrated a notable lack of familiarity with the operations of the BHA and with its performance under the consent decree.

Selection of BHA officials. The court found that the board's performance in hiring an administrator comprised a series of "almost farcical episodes." Samuel Thompson, the BHA's administrator prior to the consent decree, resigned shortly after it took effect. Initially the BHA disputed that the selection of the new administrator was subject to the procedures set forth in the consent decree. The court ruled that it was. The board appointed Kevin Feeley, general counsel to the BHA and a former purchasing agent for the city of Boston, to serve as acting administrator for three months. (The hiring provisions in the consent decree did not apply to anyone hired for three months or less.) The board then voted in January 1978 to extend his appointment for an indefinite period "until such time as a new Administrator is selected." Previously, the board had sent the master a list of five candidates they found qualified for the position. According to the provisions of the consent decree, the master conducted his own review of the candidates and found two to be highly qualified. But the board disagreed with the master's determination and decided to reinterview all five candidates. Finally, on March 6, 1978, Judge Garrity ordered the BHA to choose a permanent administrator by March 13. The board chose Bradley Biggs, one of the candidates previously approved by the master.

The position of deputy administrator also was vacant when the consent decree took effect. The master, however, agreed with the board that the administrator position should be filled first. At the first board meeting after Biggs took office, the board appointed Kevin Feeley acting deputy for ninety days. When Biggs resigned, effective October 13, 1978, the board promptly reappointed Kevin Feeley as acting administrator. Failure to reach agreement on a candidate for administrator led to a new search to fill the position. During this time Feeley and the board sought to change the administrator's job description, reducing its responsibilities. The impasse in finding a new administrator, which lasted until hearings on vacation of the consent decree had begun, left the BHA without a permanent administrator for almost half the period of the decree. Judge Garrity charged this to the board's acting "recklessly and in bad faith in its efforts to fill the top position at the BHA."

Management and operations of the BHA. The performance of the BHA in certain key areas was also criticized by Judge Garrity in his findings. For example, the BHA was unable to formulate a detailed budget and financial forecasts. Security having been a serious problem, the BHA was charged with formulating a subplan to staff and fund the security department. Instead it proposed that a blue-ribbon committee drawn from the community formulate the security program. After this proposal no more progress was made. Judge Garrity found that changes in the flow of information within the BHA seemed designed to obstruct the flow of information to the master rather than promote it. Finally, the condition of many units and common areas continued to be "appalling," widespread violations of the state sanitary code had not abated, and the vacancy rate in "family" developments (as opposed to those for the elderly) had worsened since the 1975 decision.

The Remedy: Appointment of a Receiver

On July 25, 1979, Judge Garrity ruled that receivership—supplanting the control of the board and administrator of the BHA—was the only remaining mechanism which offered a prospect (not a certainty) of moving the authority toward compliance with the sanitary code, the original goal of the litigation. In his judgment he recertified the plaintiff class to include all residential tenants of the BHA properties in which there are or may in the future be violations of the sanitary code. He vacated the consent decree and announced his intention to appoint a receiver with authority to administer, manage, and operate the BHA. The receiver was given the powers of the board of the BHA; upon his appointment the board's powers were superseded. The master was charged with submitting names of qualified candidates for receiver. An advisory committee of nine members was to be appointed with the receiver to advise him and the court.

On July 2 the board of the BHA had authorized its chair to extend all employment agreements with senior managment employees for a period of two years, ostensibly to boost employee morale. For this and other reasons the court issued several interim orders to the BHA, the master, and the plaintiffs in order to prevent "further regression" and to preserve the progress that had been made under the consent decree in moving the BHA away from a patronage-based system.

In the "July 25th decision," Judge Garrity found:

[t]he evidence introduced at the hearings . . . revealed that the Board is incapable of effective leadership and is unable and unwilling to carry out those responsibilities. The Board's incompetence and indifference to those obligations has . . . contributed not only to the BHA's failure to implement important provisions of the Consent Decree but also to the unprecedented deterioration of the BHA's developments and the widespread violations of the Sanitary Code. Throughout the four-year history of this case, the Board has shown itself to be capable of nothing more than gross mismanagement. The unabated mis- and malfeasance of the Board necessitates the extraordinary action of appointing a Receiver in this case.[13]

The Decision to Uphold the Receivership: Findings of Law

The BHA appealed the decision to the Supreme Judicial Court, which unanimously affirmed the judgment of the lower court. The higher court modified the decision only to emphasize that receivership must end as soon as feasible and to order annual hearings to be held to determine whether the receivership should be terminated.

[13]*Perez et al.* v. *Boston Housing Authority,* "Findings, Rulings, Opinion, and Orders," July 25, 1979. Commonwealth of Massachusetts Suffolk Superior Court Civil Action No. 17222.

First, the court held that the BHA, although a public body in certain respects, is submissible to and must abide by the ordinary substantive law of Massachusetts in its tenant-landlord relations.[14] In relations with tenants, the BHA has duties and rights similar to those of any landlord, including the duty to maintain its properties according to minimal standards set by the state sanitary code.[15] Thus, its liability was firmly established.

The court then noted that the more important legal problem, finding equitable remedies to ameliorate conditions at the properties to a level fit for human habitation "has proved intractable." It outlined Judge Garrity's orders from his initial resort to G.L. c. 111, section 127H (a) as the remedial instrument, that is, the court's right to issue restraining orders, preliminary injuctions, and injuctions. The appointment of the master and the issuance of interim orders stemmed from this source. When this remedy failed, the court noted, Judge Garrity resisted the step of receivership and relied again on the injunctive remedy, in the form of a consent decree.

The opinion then established the amenability of public officials to affirmative injunctions in spite of claims that these remedies both inhibit the discretion held to inhere in the offices held and pose difficult enforcement problems. The court cited *Commonwealth* v. *Hudson,* 315 Mass 335 (1943) ("municipal chlorination of water; violation of statutory obligation"); *Blaney* v. *Commissioner of Correction,* Mass (1978 [sic][16] ("treatment of prisoners in 'protective custody' status; violations of statutory standard"); and *Commonwealth* v. *Andover,* Mass. (1979) [sic][17] ("municipal revaluation of properties for tax purposes; violations of both statutory and constitutional standards"). The opinion also cited a more general trend. "On the larger scene, we may point to the extensive experience of the past quarter century with so-called 'institutional remedial litigation' (sometimes called 'extended impact' litigation), starting with the desegregation of public schools. At the center of this entire movement has been the injunctive remedial process directed to officials who have failed to abide by legal standards, commanding them to take affirmative action, often over a wide and sensitive range."[18]

The higher court upheld the superior court's power or jurisdiction to ap-

[14]See G.L. c. 121B, section 13; *Costonis* v. *Medford Housing Authority,* 322 Mass. 299, 300 (1948); *Johnston-Foster Co.* v. *D'Amore Construction Co.,* 314 Mass. 416, 419 (1943).

[15]*Boston Housing Authority* v. *Hemingway,* 363 Mass. 184 (1973).

[16]Mass. Adv. Sh. (1978) 278.

[17] Mass. Adv. Sh. (1979) 1619.

[18]Supreme Judicial Court opinion, S-1917, *Perez* v. *Boston Housing Authority,* February 4, 1980, p. 32.

point a receiver under section 127H (*a*), the provision which invokes general equity powers. "The power to compel affirmative action by injunction draws with it a power in the court to call to its assistance any agents or officers—we may call them parajudicial officers—whose services appear to be reasonably necessary to attain a legitimate objective."[19]

The BHA had appealed to put receivers in a separate class from parajudicial officers, and their appointment beyond the powers of an equity court, when their effect would be to supplant the main functions of public officials. The Supreme Judicial Court found that no such rule attaches but emphasized that receivership must be thoroughly justified on the facts, considered a "last resort," and not often applied. They stated further that as a "rule of thumb . . . the more indurated the violations of law and the remedial injunction, the more imperative and controlling the later superseding injunction."[20] With respect to public institutions the court noted:

The mechanisms at work in the creation of a neoreceivership or, in the more extreme case, a receivership of a public institution, are fairly clear. The political process has failed to produce an institution conforming to law and those subjected to the illegality, who are usually powerless . . . , turn to the courts for the vindication of their rights. Injunctive remedies are called for, but the judge lacks the expertness in the particular field, and lacks time even when he chances to have the knowledge. Hence the appointment of adjunct officers who supply expert knowledge and sometimes implicitly encourage acceptance by the parties and the general public of the results of the judicial intervention.[21]

The decision outlined the conditions that led to receivership, "massive trouble with eliciting performance of injunctive orders and finally of a comprehensive decree," and stated: "The Board cannot justly complain of being superseded when it failed, over a long period and after fair opportunity, to secure performance to the level of the injunctive orders and then the consent decree, a decree not thrust upon it but voluntarily adopted."[22]

The BHA also had argued in their appeal that receivership would offend against the principle of separation of powers. But the court dismissed this argument summarily. "[I]f it is a function of the judicial branch to provide remedies for violations of law . . . then an injunction with that intent does not

[19]Ibid., p. 34. Included in the citations are Mass. R. Civ. P. 53 (re masters), 66 (re receivers and similar officers), 365 Mass. 817, 834, 836 (1974); and the leading case, *Ex parte Peterson*, 253 U.S. 300, 312 (1920).

[20]Supreme Judicial Court opinion, S-1917, *Perez v. Boston Housing Authority*, February 4, 1980, pp. 36–37.

[21]Ibid., p. 38n.

[22]Ibid., p. 40.

derogate from the separation principle, nor, by extension, does a receivership otherwise properly instituted. . . . [I]t is the executive [in this case] that could more properly be charged with contemning the separation principle."[23]

The BHA in Receivership (1980–84)

On February 5, 1980, Judge Garrity appointed Lewis H. (Harry) Spence to be temporary receiver of the BHA and discharged Robert Whittlesey, the master, as of February 29, 1980. Under G.L. c. 111, section 127, Harry Spence was given full authority to administer, manage, and operate the BHA and control all BHA funds and revenues. Board members were prohibited from meeting or conducting any business of the BHA; using or occupying any BHA offices; removing, altering, or destroying any BHA documents; supervising any BHA employees; receiving any compensation from the BHA; or obligating or spending BHA funds.

Judge Garrity made the receiver's responsibilities explicit:

"preserve or . . . rehabilitate for occupancy . . . the maximum number of . . . units . . . ;

reduce the frequency and severity of crime, vandalism and disorder within the BHA's developments;

improve the relationship of the . . . developments to the neighborhoods in which they are located;

ensure that all residents . . . are provided equal housing opportunity consistent with legal requirements;

develop and . . . improve . . . management systems, personnel standards, employee relations and tenant relations; and

ensure, to the extent possible, that the BHA will continue to maintain and operate its developments in substantial compliance with all applicable laws after the termination of the receivership.[24]

The receiver and the plaintiffs were ordered to meet regularly with the leadership of the Tenants' Policy Council (TPC) and the plaintiffs' counsel. In addition the receiver was ordered to file a written report with the court every six months.

The court appointed the members of the Housing Advisory Committee on February 7, 1980. Their purpose was to "advise the Court and the Receiver in the formulation and implementation of Court orders" to bring the BHA's

[23]Ibid., pp. 43–44.

[24]Commonwealth of Massachusetts, Suffolk Superior Court Civil Action No. 17222, *Armando Perez et al.* v. *Boston Housing Authority,* "Order of Appointment of Receiver," February 5, 1980, p. 3.

developments into compliance with the state sanitary code. They were to meet regularly with the receiver and periodically with the court to discuss operations and any significant policy decisions. They were charged with making policy recommendations concerning the BHA's operations to Harry Spence. Judge Garrity established general rules of procedure, methods for, and frequency of reporting by the committee.

Harry Spence was successful in winning significant amounts of federal and state aid to rebuild uninhabitable developments. By 1983 nearly $175 million had been committed for both major and minor rehabilitation; the BHA had obtained funds to rehabilitate all but 360 to 400 of the 17,000 units that were vacant and uninhabitable when the receiver was appointed. In obtaining funding and restructuring management and control systems, the receivership had restored the BHA to a sound financial base. Chronically problematic tenants were evicted more often, better security was obtained at most developments, and a rate reduction for electricity sold to the BHA by Boston Edison was obtained.

But maintenance and desegregation proved to be seemingly intractable problems. Spence pledged to BHA tenants to concentrate on the maintenance problem in 1983, his third year as receiver. He cited restrictive union work rules and job descriptions in the BHA's agreement with its craft workers as the major obstacle to improved maintenance. The first attempts at desegregation came after almost four years of receivership. Nevertheless, most people agreed that Spence had been extremely successful. The lead attorney for the plaintiffs, Leslie Newman, called Spence's achievements "numerous and significant." Garrity assessed the receiver's progress as "fantastic." But a paid organizer for the tenants of the Mission Hill development criticized the receivership for continuing "a policy of neglect toward the overwhelmingly minority Mission Hill project that amounts to 'institutional racism.' "[25]

Mayor Kevin White, who had appointed most of the supplanted board members, was criticized for "abandoning" the BHA once the court took control. During the mayoral campaign preceding the 1984 election, public housing became an important issue in Boston. Boston's major daily newspaper, the *Globe*, consistently blamed Mayor White's office for Boston's housing woes. One political columnist wrote:

There's been a lot of talk recently about vacancy rates at the Boston Housing Authority. But the vacancy that matters most to the public housing residents in Boston is not in any housing project but in City Hall.

For all practical purposes, no one is at home in the mayor's office for these 50,000 Bostonians.

[25]R. S. Kindleberger, "Restructuring Hub's Public Housing," *Boston Globe*, August 20, 1983, p. 18.

Boston Mayor Kevin H. White has abandoned the BHA to the courts and has even tried to welch on the most basic city services, including police protection and garbage collection. . . .

Garrity said in an interview that he would like to see the BHA returned to political control because when it is run by the courts there is "centralized authority and almost no accountability. But," he asked, "if the BHA is returned to the political sector today, will it be raped, as it was for so many years?"

All six of the major candidates challenging White said . . . they would seek to remove the receivership and bring the BHA back under the control of the city—either of the mayor directly or through a board of directors.

But the city, under White, has made no move in that direction.[26]

In August 1983, Judge Garrity reported that he was prepared to terminate receivership at the end of its three-year duration on two conditions. He required assurances from the next Boston mayor that public housing would remain a priority after it was returned to local control. He also wanted a collective bargaining agreement between the BHA and its 350 craft wrokers which eased restrictive work rules and job descriptions, both of which he perceived as major obstacles to improved BHA maintenance. In October an agreement was reached to create twenty (semiskilled) generic maintenance worker positions. Moreover craft workers agreed to relax jurisdictional lines among some jobs so that about thirty maintenance tasks could be performed by any craft worker. In return the BHA made considerable financial concessions to the workers.

In January 1984, as Raymond Flynn prepared to take office as the new mayor of Boston, Garrity reported to the *Globe* that receivership could be lifted in late summer provided the mayor's office could institute plans to preserve the gains that had been made under the receivership.[27] However, the following month, at the annual hearing held to determine whether receivership should be terminated, the tenants and the Housing Advisory Committee requested an extension of the receivership for another year so that an orderly transition could take place. They argued that although important gains had been made, "grievous conditions" in developments remained and "weaknesses in the authority's performance continue[d] to be widespread."[28] Garrity put aside his preference for an earlier transfer and ceded to the request.

[26]Robert L. Turner, "Biggest Housing Authority Vacancy Is at City Hall," *Boston Sunday Globe*, March 6, 1983, p. A5.

[27]R. S. Kindleberger, "Court Officials Say They Expect to Get Back BHA Control," *Boston Globe*, January 7, 1984, p. 15.

[28]"BHA tenants Want Receivership Extended," *Boston Globe*, February 23, 1984, p. 22; R. S. Kindleberger, "Garrity to Control BHA for Another Year," ibid., February 25, 1984, p. 19.

Late in the summer the Flynn administration submitted a bill to the city council to restructure the BHA. In place of the relatively autonomous board of commissioners, which had made its own personnel policies and kept its own financial records, responsibility for the BHA would be put in the hands of one person, named by the mayor, whose term would be the same as the mayor's. In addition, the bill called for a nine-member monitoring commission, appointed by the mayor. Public housing tenants would hold five seats; a representative of labor and a housing expert would hold two. The annual budget of the BHA and any plans to dispose of BHA property would have to be approved by the commission. The plan was designed to give tenants a voice in operations while holding the mayor accountable overall.

On August 10, 1984, with the termination of receivership apparently pending, Harry Spence left the receiver's office. At the time of his departure a $200 million reconstruction program was underway; nearly every development in the city had established resident organizations; and a citywide organization, Tenants United for Public Housing Progress, had become politically active.

The Restorative Phase of the Receivership (1984–87)

Judge Garrity ordered the termination of the receivership and transferred the authority vested in the receiver of the BHA to Mayor Flynn on October 18, 1984. However, a new form of governance was not put in place at this time as had been planned. The form of governance put into effect when the BHA was put into receivership in 1980 was to remain in effect for two more years, during which time a new form was to be decided upon and legislated. The court action entered what Garrity called "a restorative phase" during which the plaintiff class and the court continued to monitor the progress of the BHA toward compliance with the sanitary code. The mayor was ordered to appoint a committee to assist in monitoring the performance of the BHA. Garrity outlined his view of this phase broadly.

This Court takes no formal position, nor should it, concerning the form of the BHA's future governance which is fundamentally a political issue. This court suggests that a period of experimentation occur before a final form of governance be established. A direct line of accountability between the Mayor and the BHA, with no intervening board, and a small committee with substantial tenant representation which functions solely in a monitoring capacity and has no policy role may be the most appropriate form of governance.[29]

[29]Commonwealth of Massachusetts, Suffolk Superior Court No. 17222, *Armando Perez et al. v. Boston Housing Authority*, "Findings, Rulings, and Orders," October 18, 1984, p. 26n.

Judge Garrity ruled further that the orders were to remain in effect until accomplished. A hearing was set for September 1986, at which time the court would decide whether to continue monitoring the BHA. Semiannual hearings were to continue during the interim to monitor the progress of the BHA. Judge Garrity stepped away from the case in 1984, and Judge Harry Elam of the superior court was appointed to the case. Mayor Flynn appointed Doris Bunte, a former state legislator from Roxbury, to head the BHA. By April 1986 Bunte had brought 15 percent more units up to standard than were in compliance when she assumed her role in 1984. But the executive order creating a monitoring committee was not signed until April 11, 1986, only a few months before the hearing which was supposed to terminate the receivership. Moreover, the order merely established a temporary committee. Thus, a "new form of governance" was not put in place as rapidly as expected. Tenants United for Public Housing Progress, the Committee for Public Housing, and BHA staff coordinated the establishment of the committee, which met only twice between April and November. In September 1986, because of these delays, the tenants and the BHA agreed to a one-year extension of court order which had initiated the restorative phase of the receivership. The extension was designed to allow the city to assess the feasibility of the monitoring committee.[30]

Current Status of the Case (1987)

After more than a decade, the BHA remains under court order. Shortly before the November 1986 hearing, the BHA filed a request for a three-year extension of the receivership. An attorney for the tenants, among others, saw the request as an attempt by the BHA to evade its responsibility, speculating that the authority had become more comfortable with the court's involvement than with the uncertainty of the political process.[31] The BHA quickly withdrew the request and asked the court for a one-year extension, which it granted. But Judge Elam was quoted as saying, "The court is very anxious that this case come to an end. This really doesn't belong in the court. It's been in the court long enough."[32]

In the brief filed by the plaintiffs in preparation for the hearing, BHA administrator Doris Bunte was criticized for deteriorating the relationship that had developed between the BHA and the Tenants United for Public Housing

[30]Joanne Ball, "BHA Seeks Extension of Court's Control," *Boston Globe*, November 14, 1986, p. 1ff.

[31]Ibid.

[32]Joanne Ball, "BHA Alters Request on Court Control, Asks One Year," *Boston Globe*, November 15, 1986, p. 18ff.

Progress and for refusing to meet with them. An aide to Mayor Flynn stressed the importance of cooperation between the two groups. "Greater Boston Legal Services and Tenants United are very clearly sending a message to the BHA that their relationship with the BHA could blow up. Future management of the Boston Housing Authority can't happen unless these folks are working together."[33]

Before stepping down from the case, Judge Garrity summarized the accomplishments and the continuing problems of the BHA. In many ways his assessment remains an accurate one. The BHA's ability to design programs has been greatly enhanced, but it cannot execute programs competently and in a timely manner. The BHA can now obtain and expend substantial funds successfully. Ironically, in spite of major reconstruction efforts, routine maintenance remains an intractable problem. Many buildings and apartments remain in violation of the state sanitary code. Developer and contractor compliance with construction and architectural requirements and equal opportunity requirements remain problematic. The internal organization of the BHA remains uncoordinated and insufficiently directed.

Efforts at integration have been slow and have bypassed many developments altogether. The BHA's relations with its unionized work force continue to pose serious impediments to maintenance and management improvements. The long-awaited gains made in the collective bargaining agreement negotiated in 1983 have yet to be fully implemented. The BHA now benefits from strong tenant participation. But to date no way has been found to continue the BHA's progress without court participation.

[33]Ibid.

Exhibit One: A List of the Actors in the Case

Actors Associated with the Plaintiffs

Armando Perez et al.	Eight tenants of various BHA developments originally joined with Perez as class representatives: Maria Leboy, Alejandra Montes, Mary Wellings, Margaret Gerkin, Grace O'Leary, Ruby Perkins, Linda Ferdinand, and Dolores Culbreath. Two additional tenants joined later: Pauline Morgan and Rita Driscoll.

Boston Public Housing Tenants' Policy Council, Inc.	Admitted as an intervening plaintiff.
Greater Boston Legal Services	Agency representing the plaintiffs.
Leslie Newman	Lead attorney for the plaintiffs.
Tenants United for Public Housing Progress	Citywide tenants' organization, emerged during receivership period.

Actors Associated with the Defendants

The Boston Housing Authority	The defendant.
Board of Commissioners	Five-member body responsible for managing, controlling, and governing the BHA, whose powers were supplanted by receivership: Barbara Carpenter, chair; John Battos; Otto Snowden; Patrick Moscaritolo (one seat vacant).
Samuel Thompson	Administrator, resigned, 10/77.
Kevin Feeley	Acting administrator, 10/77–3/78, 10/78–2/80; acting deputy administrator, 3–10/78.
Bradley Biggs	Administrator, 3–10/78.
Doris Bunte	Administrator appointed by Mayor Flynn, 10/84–present (1987).
Kevin H. White	Mayor of Boston, 1966–84.
Raymond L. Flynn	Mayor of Boston, 1984–present (1987).
Monitoring Committee	Nine-person body appointed by Mayor Flynn to monitor BHA and advise the administrator.

Actors Associated with the Court

Paul Garrity	Presided over case while Boston Housing Court justice; continued to preside over case as superior court justice, 1976–84.

Harry Elam	Superior court justice presiding over the case, 1984–present (1987).
Robert Whittlesey	Court-appointed master of the BHA, 5/22/75–2/29/80.
Lewis H. (Harry) Spence	Court-appointed receiver of the BHA, 2/5/80–10/18/84.
John Stainton	Acting receiver of the BHA, 9–10/84.
Housing Advisory Council	Nine-member committee appointed by the court to advise it and the receiver; Robert Kiley (chair), Dorothy Bambach, Anna Blassingame, Robert Gardner, Charles Haar, James Hoyte, Roderick Ireland, Lyda Peters, Rev. Robert Quinn, Alan Root, Byron Rushing, Maria Sanchez, Daniel Sullivan.
Supreme Judicial Court	Unanimously upheld order for receivership.

Other Actors

Citizens Housing and Planning Committee	Nonprofit organization of Boston residents, tenants, and public officials to promote better housing for low- and moderate-income people and to improve community planning and development.
United States Department of Housing and Urban Planning	Supervisory agency to the BHA.
Office of Economic and Community Development	Supervisory agency to the BHA.
The *Boston Globe*	Boston newspaper, major actor for the media.

Appendix 4 *Connecticut Association for Retarded Citizens et al. v. Thorne et al.* United States District Court, District of Connecticut

Case history prepared by Paula J. Caproni

Summary

In December 1978, the Connecticut Association for Retarded Citizens (CARC), a group of parents and advocates of mentally retarded individuals living in Connecticut, filed a claim against Gareth Thorne et al. on behalf of twelve residents of Mansfield Training School (MTS). They challenged the appropriateness and adequacy of conditions, care, habilitation, and residential placement for mentally retarded persons residing at MTS and those who had been transferred from MTS to long-term care facilities. CARC charged that the defendants had violated plaintiffs' federal constitutional and statutory rights and requested, by way of relief, that the defendants be ordered to provide class members with adequate physical care, individualized habilitation programs, and residential placements in community settings appropriate to their needs. In addition, CARC requested, and received, certification as a class action suit, representing approximately 1,433 individuals, including the more than 859 retarded people living at MTS, retarded people for whom MTS was responsible but who were living in nursing homes across the state, and several people who were at risk of being committed to MTS.

After four years of bitter pretrial discovery, several months of negotiations, and six days of trial testimony, CARC, the U.S. Justice Department, and the state settled out of court by negotiating and agreeing to a consent decree on May 25,

1983. After thirty-one days of fairness hearings on the original proposed consent decree, during which time both the Mansfield Parents Association (MPA) and New England Health Care Employees Union, District 1199, intervened in opposition to the proposed consent decree, a one-day hearing on the modified proposed consent decree, a two-day tour of Mansfield Training School, tours of various other facilities for the mentally retarded, all parties, with the exception of the union, agreed to and signed the modified proposed consent decree on November 7, 1983.

The modified proposed consent decree mandated reduction of the population at MTS, as well as at skilled nursing facilities, and the development of community residential placements for individual plaintiffs and class members. Interdisciplinary individualized evaluations were required for each client regarding appropriate habilitation and placement, with substantial weight to be given to the views of class members and parents, family members, guardians, or advocates. All class members, regardless of the nature or severity of their handicap, were to be equally eligible for community placement. Defendants were required to hire sufficient professional staff to meet the programming needs set forth in the consent decree. They were also required to provide appropriate training for personnel involved in the habilitative and community placement process, as well as for direct care staff.

The consent decree mandated that all residential facilities and program and staff standards would at least minimally comply with Intermediate Care Facility/Mental Retardation [ICF/MR] standards, and provisions were included for the maintenance of a safe and sanitary environment. Physical and psychological abuse was prohibited, and physical restraints and psychotropic medication could no longer be employed without a written comprehensive behavioral treatment plan.

The decree mandated the appointment of four court monitors and the development, by the defendants with approval of the plaintiffs, of a comprehensive implementation plan. CARC and MPA were given advisory and problem-solving responsibility with respect to the implementation of conditions set forth in the consent decree.

Chronology

This chronology is based primarily on the Joint Proposed Findings of Fact submitted to the court in January 1984.

December 6, 1978. CARC and several named plaintiffs file complaint challenging adequacy and appropriateness of conditions, care, habilitation, and residential placement for mentally retarded persons residing at MTS and those who had been transferred from MTS to long-term care facilities. They

charge that defendants had violated plaintiffs' alleged rights under certain
federal constitutional and statutory provisions and requested, by way of
relief, that the defendants be ordered to provide class members with individualized habilitation programs and residential placement in community settings appropriate to their needs.

September 13, 1979. Mansfield Parents Association (MPA) et al. move to
intervene to oppose class certification, to oppose any attempt to close MTS,
and to take necessary steps to protect rights and interests of retarded citizens
in Connecticut to have a full range of treatment facilities available that are
appropriate to each person's individual condition and need.

December 13, 1979. U.S. Justice Department moves to participate at litigating
amicus curiae "to conduct discovery, present witnesses at trial, and make
oral arguments on its behalf."

February 8, 1980. Motion of U.S. Justice Department granted.

February 8, 1980. Motion of MPA granted.

February 8, 1980. Court certifies action as class action to include all persons
who reside at MTS or may be transferred there in the future; retarded persons
residing at home who are in jeopardy of being sent to MTS; and persons who
have been transferred to skilled nursing facilities; intermediate care facilities,
homes for the aged, and similar facilities yet who remain the responsibility of
MTS.

April 3, 1980. New England Health Care Employees Union, District 1199,
moves to intervene in this case to protect any interests of its members that
may be affected by the outcome of this litigation. District 1199 files a cross-
complaint seeking to enjoin the defendants from implementing changes
which are contrary to the provisions of collective bargaining agreements or
which would violate the provisions of 42 U.S.C.S. 67063 (b)(7)(b).

July 7, 1980. Motion for District 1199 to intervene granted.

Early 1979–early 1983. Plaintiffs, defendants, and U.S. Justice Department
engage in extensive discovery including numerous interrogatories and requests for production, nearly one hundred depositions, and tours of MTS,
community residential facilities, and long-term care facilities by approximately forty-five expert witnesses.

February 8, 1983. Four months of "difficult, intensive, and arms-length" negotiations toward consent decree begin.

February 13, 1983. Plaintiff's initial settlement proposal sent to Deputy Attorney General Elliot Gerson requesting the appointment of a special master.

May 6, 1983. Trial of case is referred to Honorable F. Owen Eagan, U.S.
magistrate, by order of Judge Emmet Clarie upon stipulation of all parties.

May 9, 1983. Trial on the merits of the case commences, followed by six days of
trial testimony and a two-day magistrate's tour of MTS.

May 25, 1983. Plaintiffs, defendants, and U.S. Justice Department agree on proposed consent decree.

May 26, 1983. Governor O'Neill, plaintiffs, and defendants hold press conference to applaud the signing of the proposed consent decree.

May 27, 1983. Plaintiffs, defendants and U.S. Justice Department submit proposed consent decree to the court.

May 31, 1983. Court determines the proposed consent decree is of sufficient content and legal merit to warrant notice to class members. Glossary of terms becomes part of decree. Hundreds of letters from class members, families of class members, and other interested individuals and organizations are received, reflecting a range of support of and objections to the proposed consent decree.

June 12, 1983. Intervenors MPA file memorandum voicing a number of objections to the decree, questioning the relief requested by the plaintiffs.

June 27, 1983. Upon request of the plaintiffs, court conducts a one-day tour of selected community residential and day programs in Connecticut.

July 1, 1983. Court conducts one-day tour of selected community residents and day-care facilities in Massachusetts.

July 1, 1983. Intervenors 1199 file formal statement of objections urging disapproval of proposed consent decree on the grounds that they were not directly included in negotiation process and that, in their opinion, the decree was too vague on a number of important issues.

July 12, 1983. Court conducts one-day tour of selected community residential and day-care facilities in New York.

July 12, 1983. Intervenors MPA file memorandum in objection to proposed consent decree stating as their primary areas of concern their lack of direct involvement in the negotiation process and their belief that CARC does not adequately represent the interests of class members at MTS, that the proposed consent decree gave too little weight and due process protections to the views and concerns of parents of class members and other interested family members, and that the proposed consent decree did not afford them the opportunity to participate in the monitor selection process or to act as an adviser to the defendants during implementation.

July 13, 1983. Fairness hearings commence for purpose of all interested parties to present evidence to assist the court in ruling on the proposed consent decree.

November 7, 1983. Plaintiffs, defendants, U.S. Justice Department, and MPA sign and submit modified proposed consent decree.

November 16, 1983. Notice on modified proposed consent decree is sent to appropriate parties requiring that all written objections be filed with the court no later than December 16, 1983.

December 17, 1983. New England Health Care Employees Union, District 1199, files formal statement of objections.

December 22, 1983. Hearing is held concerning any objections to modified proposed consent decree.

April 9, 1984. Modified proposed consent decree signed by Magistrate Eagan.

History before Litigation

History of Mansfield Training School

In 1858, Connecticut School for Imbeciles was established in Lakeville in order to "educate individuals who, because of their handicapping conditions, were unable to effectively use community-based educational facilities."[1] The population at the School for Imbeciles grew from 15 in 1858 to 304 students in 1915. In 1917, following a state report titled "The Menace of the Feeble-Minded at Large in Connecticut," a eugenics scare, and the state legislature's allocation of $200,000, the School for Imbeciles was combined with the Connecticut Colony for Epileptics to inform a new facility in Mansfield, known today as Mansfield Training School. The superintendent of the School for Imbeciles explained the purpose of this expansion was to

stop the supply of the vicious, the weak, the no-willed people who cannot support themselves in the community—of the criminals and prostitutes and paupers, by cutting off the supply at its source, namely—by providing adequate custodial care for the feeble minded of the state. This is especially important in the case of women of child-bearing age. Admission to the Lakeville School has been sought for many of this class during the past year, but there was no room for them.[2]

In a 1918 report to the governor, Mansfield's purpose was declared to be "the training and socialization of each and every one of its patients; to eliminate asocial and other undesirable habits and to bring out and develop in the individual patients all abilities that will help to make the patient as nearly self-supporting as possible and return to the community all who are socially and industrially fit."[3] The population of MTS in 1934 was 1,159, with a waiting list of 1,073. A second institution, Southbury Training School, was established in 1941.

In the 1950s, Connecticut began to consider community alternatives to the

---

[1]"Report of the Commissioner on Idiocy," 1856. "CARC Findings of Fact," 1984.

[2]"The Menace of the Feeble-Minded at Large in Connecticut," 1915. "CARC Findings of Fact," 1984.

[3]"Report to the Governor, Mansfield Training School and Hospital for the Two-Year Period Ending September 30, 1918." "CARC Findings of Fact," 1984.

total institutionalization of individuals who were labeled mentally retarded and began to develop a community service network. During this decade, the first state-operated day-care center was opened in Hartford; private day programs emerged; the legislature mandated the provision of special education to children up to age twenty-one; the Office of Mental Retardation was established within the State Department of Health; and twelve regional centers were developed throughout the state, the primary purpose of which was to provide support and assistance to the disabled and families of the disabled in the community.

During the 1960s, Connecticut gained a reputation as an innovative leader in the field of mental retardation. Nationally, the Kennedy initiatives, several acts of Congress, and professional attitudes reflected an awareness of the rights of the mentally retarded and their potential for growth. In 1967, however, the nation reached its peak in the institutionalization of the mentally retarded. Mansfield reflected this trend, reaching a peak population of two thousand in the midsixties.

By the 1970s, as a result of the human rights movements of the 1960s, changes in federal standards, and several suits filed throughout the nation challenging the quality and appropriateness of care at state institutions, there was a gradual reduction in the institutionalization of the mentally retarded. In 1973, Gareth Thorne, commissioner of Connecticut's Department of Mental Retardation, introduced the state's planning document, "Project Challenge," which set forth the state's long-range goal of reducing the rate of institutionalization while concurrently developing home-style living arrangements and support systems in the community. In this document, Thorne stated:

There is no simple answer to planning a future for more than 45,000 mentally retarded people in Connecticut; but the courts of the land, and the people who have given great thought to this issue—not only the parents but the professionals as well, have strongly indicated and pressured a course of action which ensures the rights of the mentally handicapped person to live in partnership with his fellow beings. To make any other decision would be to turn away from this central issue and to thereby seek expedient means for avoiding a major social and legal responsibility. . . . The problem basically is that outmoded institutions exist, and every effort must be made to resolve this problem and to prevent it from occurring again by literally tearing outmoded facilities down brick by brick until nothing remains and in this process bring the handicapped person back home to the community where he belongs.[4]

Project Challenge was revised in August 1976, February 1978, and October 1978.

[4]"Project Challenge: The Long-Range Plan of the Office of Mental Retardation," 1973.

The Office of Mental Retardation began licensing private residential facilities for the mentally retarded, and the Federal Intermediate Care Facility for the Mentally Retarded program was officially begun in Connecticut. In 1975, the office of mental retardation became a separate state agency, the Department of Mental Retardation. Federal funds under the Title XIX program were used to develop community residential alternatives to accommodate some of the over one thousand persons who were scheduled to return to the community.

Despite the nationwide trend toward deinstitutionalization and Connecticut's own stated commitment to community-based care through Project Challenge, the state remained deeply embedded in the institutional model of care. According to Dr. David Braddock, "I believe what has happened is Connecticut took a very progressive stance in the 1960s in an effort to reform its institutions and became overcommitted to the institutional model of providing services."[5]

The state's progress was slow in developing the community-based homes and programs. This delay was attributed to budgetary constraints; bureaucratic red tape in the purchase, leasing, and/or construction of community facilities; and the bureaucratic complexities involved in redirecting a complicated, highly invested, institutional service system to an even more complicated community-based service model. Efforts toward deinstitutionalization and the development of community residences and habilitation, and treatment programs were also hampered by the ambivalence and resistance of groups within the state leadership, the professional communities, the state employees, parent and advocacy groups, the receiving communities, and the residential community of the state hospitals and long-term care facilities.

By 1978, when CARC et al. filed their claim against Gareth Thorne et al., the state of Connecticut had created the Mansfield and Southbury training schools, housing 1,017 and 1,242 residents respectively, and twelve regional centers with populations ranging from 25 to 255. In addition, the state had placed 310 people in 28 state-funded group homes and 839 people in nursing homes throughout the state.

In the early 1980s, Connecticut had the second highest rate of institutionalization of retarded citizens in the nation, surpassed only by North Dakota, which at the time was also under a court order. Connecticut was spending more per capita on its institutions than any other state.

The Decision to Litigate

In the late 1970s, several parents of MTS residents sought legal assistance from David Shaw, legal aid society lawyer, over their concerns with the quality of

[5]*The Day,* New London, Connecticut, November 11, 1984.

care and treatment provided to their sons and daughters residing at MTS. Having attempted to improve the quality of care and to obtain educational services and programs without success, the parents, together with attorney Shaw, felt the time was right for bringing a suit against the state. Fully 80–90 percent of the state's Department of Mental Retardation resources were going to state institutions. The more parents and advocates complained about the conditions and treatment at MTS, the more resources were invested in the institution. "It seemed," according to attorney Shaw, "to be a bottomless pit." Nationally, state institutions for the mentally retarded were embroiled in a number of legal battles challenging the quality and appropriateness of the institutionalized services provided to the mentally retarded. *Normalization, communitization,* and *deinstitutionalization* became the buzzwords of the decade. The nation's administration and legal system leaned favorably toward the newer models of institutional reform.

CARC is a nonprofit organization with a membership of approximately six thousand families statewide. The stated purpose of CARC at that time was "to promote the general welfare of mentally retarded persons in the State of Connecticut."[6] Attorney Shaw and the parents approached CARC, as well as other advocacy groups, with their concerns about MTS and the idea of the lawsuit. CARC requested that attorney Shaw submit a proposal highlighting what the suit would seek to accomplish. After a few divisive meetings, CARC voted to join the suit. Three local chapters of the CARC—Bridgeport, Stamford, and New London—left the group in opposition. CARC, because of its role as community service providers, was accused of using the suit for financial benefit. The state was accused of providing more assistance to ARCs which did not support the lawsuit. Bridgeport withdrew $20,000 in membership fees when it withdrew its membership.

The United Cerebral Palsy Association and Connecticut Society for Autistic Children chose not to join. Advocacy groups which were service providers as well as advocates for the handicapped were concerned that such a suit might "bite the hand that fed them." At that time, United Cerebral Palsy Association was getting money from the state. They later publicly supported the suit.

The Complaint

Summary of Complaint

In December 1978, CARC filed a complaint on behalf of twelve individual plaintiffs residing at Mansfield Training School against Gareth Thorne and

[6]Ibid.

four other state officials "to redress the unconstitutional conditions imposed on persons incarcerated by the State of Connecticut in Mansfield Training School, (Mansfield) and to declare and enforce the constitutional and statutory rights of retarded persons to effective services in an integrated community setting."[7]

The original plaintiffs requested, and received, certification as a class action, representing approximately 1,433 individuals, including those living at Mansfield Training School, those for whom MTS was responsible but who were living in nursing homes across the state, and several people who were at risk of being committed to MTS. The complaint asserted claims under the First, Fourth, Fifth, Ninth, and Fourteenth amendments to the U.S. Constitution and sections of the Rehabilitation Act of 1973, the Social Security Act, and the Developmentally Disabled Assistance and Bill of Rights Act.

They sought "declaratory and injunctive relief to require defendants to create the quantity and type of community living arrangements and other community services necessary for the habilitation of all plaintiffs and class-members in the least separate, most integrated, least restrictive community setting."[8] See exhibit 2 for a more detailed account of the plaintiffs' original claims. The complaint was based on the principle of normalization, "a fundamental, widely accepted principle in the treatment of mentally retarded persons. It is based on the recognition of retarded persons as full human beings with rights to liberty and self-actualization; and on the practical experience and observation that retarded persons can best achieve these goals in life patterns which are integrated with and similar to those followed by other persons."[9]

Main Issues

Nearly everyone involved says all the groups have the same goal—to improve the lives of the state's retarded residents. (*Hartford Courant,* May 27, 1984)

At issue is whether there is a need for Mansfield Training School at all—and state officials say there is a need, however limited—and how quickly the move to community based facilities should take place. (*Willimantic Chronicle,* May 16, 1983)

---

[7]"Original Complaint," 1978. The other defendants were Roger MacNamara, superintendent of MTS; Francis Maloney, commissioner of the Connecticut Department of Children and Youth Services; Edward Maher, commissioner of the Connecticut Department of Social Services; and Douglas Lloyd, commissioner of the Connecticut Department of Health.

[8]Ibid.

[9]Ibid.

No retarded person needs Mansfield Training School because of his handicaps. Mansfield is harmful to retarded citizens. ("CARC Findings of Fact," 1978)

As the pressure to deinstitutionalize increases, so do fears. Many parents envision their retarded children being forced into an outside world that has little use for them, with inadequate services but many dangers. (*The Day,* New London, Connecticut, November 11, 1984)

Overall, the purpose of CARC's claim was to change the state's current system for caring for and providing services to the mentally retarded from one which had virtually the highest per capita rate of institutionalization for any state in the nation to one which would be based in community residences and support systems.

All parties agreed that the best interest of the class members should be at the heart of the suit and that the state of Connecticut should be committed to providing the best possible care to mentally retarded individuals living in Connecticut. The parties differed, however, over the theory of care. While the CARC asserted that "proper rehabilitation of mentally retarded [could not] be carried out in an institution"[10] that residential and day services for the mentally retarded, as well as support services for families of the mentally retarded, were best offered in the community, the defendants asserted that proper care of the mentally retarded required a range of alternatives, including the alternatives provided by the continued existence of MTS.

The Mansfield Parents Association bitterly opposed CARC's efforts toward deinstitutionalization, claiming that the class action suit was not representing the will of everyone in the class. The Mansfield Parents Association, composed primarily of older parents with adult children who had been institutionalized for years, had invested much of their lives in maintaining and improving the quality of life at MTS. They were fearful that community placement might be detrimental to their children. The CARC parents and advocates were younger and had younger children. Having felt the benefit of legislation which had entitled their children to an education, and having had more experience with community support systems, they were more aware of the alternatives to institutionalization, had higher expectations of what their children could accomplish, and were optimistic about the possibilities for a community-based residential and service network for the mentally retarded.

The divisiveness between the parties in the suit did not stop at the ideological level. Practical concerns—such as the cost of institutional versus community-based care—were used to support the parties' positions. They could not agree on the comparative costs of institutionally based and

[10]Ibid.

community-based residences for the mentally retarded. The state produced evidence that community placement would cost approximately $52,000 per person per year. Margaret Dignoti of the CARC produced evidence that the community-based system might be more expensive during the initial transition from institutionalized to community residences, yet the cost of living in the community would average out to $41,000 per person per year. James Conroy, director of research and evaluation at Temple University, later testified, based on a seven-year study in Pennsylvania, that annual "social costs for patients in community living arrangements were $7,000 less than expenses for those who remained in traditional institutions. But it is possible that costs to taxpayers can increase if deinstutionalization is not carried out properly." His Pennsylvania study indicated that costs for people who remained in the institution averaged $47,170, whereas costs for individuals who moved to community placements averaged $40,284. He noted, however, that the state's share of costs for people in the community increased from 45.4 percent (institution) to 88.7 percent (community).[11]

The Discovery Period and Suspended Trial

From early 1979 through early 1983, the parties engaged in an exhaustive and bitter pretrial discovery period. This discovery period included "numerous interrogatories and requests for production, nearly 100 depositions, and tours of MTS, community residential facilities, and long-term care facilities by approximately 45 expert witnesses."[12] Lack of trust, confidence, and civility plagued the discovery process. While most of the bitterness was attributed to the accusations and recriminations that parties exchanged throughout the process, it has also been suggested that Connecticut's New England culture played a role in the escalating animosity.[13]

In September 1979, the MPA moved to intervene to oppose class certification, to oppose any attempt to close MTS, and to take necessary steps to protect the rights and interests of retarded citizens to receive a full range of treatment facilities. This motion was granted in February 1980.[14]

[11]Testimony of James Conroy, director of research and evaluation at Temple University.

[12]"Joint Findings of Fact," January 1984.

[13]Connecticut folk wisdom predicts that the people of Connecticut will respond particularly unfavorably to a lawsuit (say, in comparison to the people of New York or Pennsylvania). This unfavorable response has been attributed to a greater tendency to take things personally and to a dislike of outsider intervention in personal and state matters.

[14]"Joint Findings of Fact," January, 1984. Quotations in the following three paragraphs are from this same source.

In December 1979, the U.S. Justice Department moved to participate as litigating amicus curiae "to conduct discovery, present witnesses at trial, file briefs, and make oral arguments on its behalf." The motion was granted in February 1980. The Justice Department's entry in the case on the side of the plaintiffs provided financial leverage, credibility, and a morale boost to the plaintiffs.

In February 1980, the court certified the action as a class action to include "all persons who reside at MTS or may be transferred there in the future; retarded persons residing at home who are in jeopardy of being sent to MTS; and persons who have been transferred to skilled nursing facilities, intermediate care facilities, homes for the aged, and similar facilities yet who remain Mansfield's responsibility."

In April 1980, "the New England Health Care employees Union, District 1199, moved to intervene in this case to protect any interests of its members that may be affected by the outcome of the litigation." This motion was granted in July 1980. At the same time, the union filed a cross-complaint seeking to enjoin the defendants from implementing changes which are contrary to the provisions of collective bargaining agreements or which would violate the provisions of 42 U.S.C.S 6063 (b)(7)(b).

In early 1983, six Mansfield aides were arrested and charged with cruelty to the residents. This event was of symbolic value to both the plaintiffs and the defendants. While the plaintiffs considered the cruel behavior to be an extreme, but nonetheless representative, example of the treatment of institutionalized individuals, the defendants argued that the arrested employees' behavior was a result of underfunding and understaffing and that such behavior was not an inherent feature of institutional life.

From February 8, 1983, through May 25, 1983, the plaintiffs, the defendants, and the U.S. Justice Department engaged in heated negotiations regarding the provisions of a proposed consent decree. During this time, on May 9, 1983, the trial on the merits commenced, presided by the Honorable F. Owen Eagan, U.S. magistrate, by order of Judge Emmet Claire. Early in May, the U.S. Justice Department and the state reached agreement on the proposed consent decree. This agreement between the Justice Department and the state was a critical point in the negotiations, for with that agreement CARC lost the support and leverage provided by the Justice Department. The *Hartford Courant* reported, "[The Justice Department] had been the major backer of the suit, and if that support is withdrawn with the department siding publicly with the State, it could effectively end the suit."[15]

On May 25, 1983, after six days of the trial on the merits of the case, the

[15]*Hartford Courant,* May 24, 1983.

hearing of the testimony of five witnesses, and a two-day tour of the facility, the plaintiffs, defendants, and the U.S. Justice Department reached an agreement with respect to the proposed consent decree. The trial was suspended.

Although the negotiations reflected "the difficult, intensive, and arms-length" relationships that had existed throughout the pretrial discovery period, all parties agreed that settling out of court with a consent decree had saved everybody a long, costly, and bitter trial on the merits. It was estimated that a full trial on the merits would have taken at least seven months, excluding the presentation of evidence by any intervenors. The parties had listed approximately 90 expert witnesses and 200 exhibits, defendants had listed 703 exhibits, and the U.S. Justice Department listed 226 nonexpert witnesses, excluding possible rebuttal witnesses. Plaintiffs had listed 1,036 exhibits.[16]

The defendants concluded that by negotiating and agreeing to a consent decree, "they traded a trial with an uncertain outcome for a plan the Department of Mental Retardation endorses which allows the state to retain control over the administration of its programs and sets no figures on the number of people who must be deinstutionalized, or by what time."[17] The plaintiffs also concluded that a negotiated consent decree was better than an uncertain outcome of a trial. The discovery period had dragged on four and one-half years, and during that time the new administration and courts in the nation began to show less sympathy toward the deinstitutionalization movement. All parties agreed that the time spent on the trial could be best used in advancing the quality of care and services provided to the mentally retarded in the state.

On May 26, 1983, the plaintiffs and defendants joined Governor O'Neill in a carefully staged press conference at the state capital. However, the tension which had grown between the parties did not subside with the signing of the proposed consent decree. On May 27, the *Hartford Courant* reported:

The warring parties appeared for a show of solidarity Thursday when Gov. William A. O'Neill formally announced the settlement of a lawsuit against the Mansfield Training School, but underlying tensions showed through. . . . Despite Attorney General Joseph I. Lieberman's statement that "division and suspicion will be set aside" the first sign of differences emerged during the news conference as Mental Retardation Commissioner Gareth D. Thorne fielded questions from reporters.

Asked about the cost of creating group homes for the retarded people who now live at Mansfield and in nursing homes, Thorne said $5 million would be spent next year to build 20 group homes, and he would ask for another $5 million the following year. Then association president Quincy S. Abbot jumped

16"Joint Proposed Findings of Fact," January 1984.
17*Hartford Courant*, May 26, 1983.

in. "The cost is cheaper in the community and the quality of life is better" said Abbot, arguing the association's long-held position that group homes cost less than large institutions, a position with which Thorne disagrees. And Abbot continued to step in and offer his own answers to questions reporters were asking Thorne. "I just couldn't let him get by with saying some of those things," Abbot, who has a moderately retarded daughter, said afterward as he explained why he kept interjecting despite Thorne's irritation.

Throughout the news conference, the room swirled with muttered opinions from the crowd of onlookers, some objecting to statements made by state officials, others sarcastically sneering at Abbot's remarks.

The Mansfield Parents Association, although they signed the modified proposed consent decree, were still at odds with CARC. They continued to support the existence of MTS, while CARC hoped the consent decree would lead to an eventual closing of the institution. Roger MacNamara, MTS superintendent, added to the tension by publicly, though cautiously, expressing support for deinstitutionalization. The MPA felt betrayed by the superintendent with whom they had worked so closely over the years. Commissioner Thorne made it clear to the press that MacNamara's comments expressed his personal opinion and did not reflect the opinion of Commissioner Thorne or the Department of Mental Retardation.

On May 31, 1983, the court determined that the proposed consent decree was of significant content and merit to warrant notice to class members. In response to the notice, hundreds of letters were received. Class members, families of class members, and other interested parties wrote to express their support of or objections to the consent decree. Those who supported the consent decree urged immediate implementation. Those who opposed the consent decree objected to the lack of participation of the MPA and certain provisions of the consent decree.[18]

On June 12, intervenors MPA filed a memorandum in which they expressed their objections to the proposed consent decree, questioning the relief requested by the named plaintiffs. Their primary areas of concern were "their lack of direct involvement in the negotiation process, their belief that CARC [did] not adequately represent the interests of class members at MTS, that the proposed consent decree gave too little weight and due process protections to the views and concerns of parents of classmembers and other interested family members, and that the proposed consent decree did not afford them the opportunity to participate in the monitor selection process or to act as an advisor to the defendants during implementation." On July 1, intervenors District 1199 filed a formal statement of objections disapproving of the decree on the

---

[18]"Joint Findings of Fact," November 1983.

grounds that they were not involved during negotiations and that the consent decree was too vague on a number of important issues.[19]

The court conducted one-day tours of selected community residential and day programs in Connecticut, Massachusetts, and New York on June 27, July 1, and July 12 respectively. On July 13, 1983, fairness hearings on the consent decree commenced for the purpose of allowing all interested parties to present evidence to assist the court in ruling on whether the proposed consent decree should be approved. The hour from 4:00 to 5:00 P.M. was reserved each day of the hearing for interested members of the general public to testify under oath regarding their interests in the proceedings and their views on the proposed consent decree.

On November 7, 1983, the plaintiffs, defendants, U.S. Department of Justice, and the intervenors MPA et al. reached agreement on and signed a modified proposed consent decree. From November 16 through December 16, following an order of notice on the modified proposed consent decree, only eight letters were received regarding the decree. Four of these letters were from family members who did not object to the modified proposed consent decree but who wanted their family member to stay at MTS; one letter expressed the view that the lawsuit was unnecessary and a waste of money; two letters primarily expressed their objections to CARC's conduct throughout the case; and one letter applauded the consent decree. No parents of the named plaintiffs objected to the consent decree, and in none of the eight letters were there objections to substantive provisions of the modified proposed consent decree.[20]

District 1199, however, still opposed the consent decree and filed a formal statement of objections, citing the following:

(a) Appearance of conflict of interest with CARC as the class representative

(b) Modified Consent Decree continues to be vague and ambiguous

(c) District 1199 was not included in negotiations leading up to MPCD

(d) Decree should provide for clearer standards to be imposed on private operators of community facilities

(e) Staffing requirements of the Decree are inadequate

(f) Court should appoint independent advocates for each classmember who does not have an involved close relative or guardian.[21]

[19]Ibid.
[20]Ibid.
[21]"Joint Findings of Fact," January 1984.

On December 22, at the modified proposed consent decree hearing, only District 1199 expressed objections to the decree, calling Commissioner Thorne and Union President Jerry Brown to testify regarding the decree. District 1199 objectives were ruled unfounded.

On April 9, 1984, the modified proposed consent decree was signed by Magistrate Eagan. Under the consent decree, the state agreed to certain terms which could be enforced by the court, including the appointment of four court monitors for a minimum period of four years. By signing the consent decree, the plaintiffs relinquished their right to appeal in a higher court.

The Consent Decree

Summary of the Modified Proposed Consent Decree

"Given the number of parties involved in this litigation, the size of the class, the unique circumstances of each individual classmember, the emotionalism sur- rounding the issues involved in the case and the unfortunate bitterness and mistrust that has plagued the parties throughout this litigation, the reaction of classmembers, their families, and other interested persons and organizations to the proposed consent decree of November 7, 1983 is nothing short of remark- able."[22] The modified proposed consent decree required reduction of the popu- lation at MTS, as well as at skilled nursing facilities, and the development of community residential placements for MTS clients. Interdisciplinary individu- alized evaluations were required for each client regarding appropriate habilita- tion and placement, with substantial weight given to the views of class mem- bers and parents, family members, guardians, or advocates. All class members, regardless of the nature or severity of their handicap, were to be equally eligible for community placement. All class members were to be provided with hab- ilitative programs and services deemed appropriate to their needs by the inter- disciplinary team. Appropriate training for personnel involved in the habilita- tive and community placement procedures was required. The defendants were required to provide sufficient professional staff to meet the programming needs set forth in the consent decree, as well as appropriate training for direct care staff.

In addition, the consent decree mandated that all residential facilities and program and staff standards would at a minimum comply with court-approved standards, and provisions were included for the the maintenance of a safe and sanitary environment. Physical and psychological abuse was prohibited, and

---

[22]Ibid.

physical restraints and psychotropic medication could be employed only in conjunction with a written comprehensive behavioral treatment plan.

The decree mandated the appointment of four court monitors and the development, by the defendants with approval of plaintiffs, of a comprehensive implementation plan. The CARC and MPA were given advisory and problem-solving responsibility with respect to the implementation of the provisions of the consent decree.[23]

Overall, the decree did not focus on detail. While the plaintiffs had hoped the decree would require specific substantive changes, it instead focused largely on the process of change. CARC did not get the commitment to the development of small-group homes of six people or less, nor did they get a commitment to a specific number of placements or a guarantee to close the institution. They did succeed in pushing systemic changes which would channel MTS's and the Department of Mental Retardation's process to come out in favor of community placement. The successful implementation of the consent decree depended largely upon the good faith of the defendants, the implementation plan developed by the defendants, the relationships among the parties involved, the judgments of the state's professionals, and the role played by the court monitors.

Court-Appointed Monitors

The responsibilities of the court monitors are (1) to monitor compliance with the decree; (2) to consult with counsel of the department and the plaintiffs "on any dispute involving the interpretation, enforcement or modification" of the decree; and (3) to report to the court and the parties "regarding compliance."[24] The true nature of the board of monitors did not become apparent until after the decree was formulated. The monitors immediately acquired two roles: a formal policing role stemming from the terms of the consent decree and an informal, but equally powerful and important, mediating role stemming from the need to repair the brittle relationships that had developed throughout the five-year battle. The signing of the consent decree did not mend the sore relationships among the parties, yet the spirit and success of the decree relied on collaboration and good faith.

In their policing role, the monitors had the responsibility for monitoring compliance with the consent decree and had access to individual plaintiffs and class members, staff, and official documents. However, according to Mr. Lottman, executive director of the court monitors, nobody, including the monitors,

[23]Modified Proposed Consent Decree, November 1983.
[24]"CARC v. *Thorne* Consent Decree Implementation Plan," August 1985.

knew exactly what level of authority the monitors had. In response to this ambiguity, the monitors chose to assume a position of authority, and this position was, overall, respected by the plaintiffs and the defendants.

Aside from the implementation plan and a longitudinal study, the court required no other reports from the defendants or the monitors. The monitors, however, required reports on all client movements, incident reports of alleged abuse and use of mechanical restraints, copies of ICF/MR surveys done on the progress of class members, and monthly reports on Bennett Hall, which, as a result of citations during a Health Department survey, had been removed from the Medicaid Program in October 1984, costing $360,000 per quarter in Medicaid reimbursements. They also conducted on-site audits of all placements and investigated complaints by plaintiffs and parents.

In their mediating role, the monitors relied as often as possible on negotiations between the parties and consensus decision making. The monitors, the plaintiffs, and the defendants realized that the last thing the magistrate wanted was for the case repeatedly to be before the court.

Regarding the role of the monitors, a note in the *Yale Law Journal* stated:

The monitors' ability to induce cooperation may be impaired however, by two characteristics which differentiate them from mediators. First, they are not called in to arrange a compromise between conflicting interests; rather, their purpose is the furtherance of objectives already laid down by the court. Second, they can and do resort to judicial compulsion when their recommendations are not adopted. Endowed with these policeman-like attributes, monitors cannot successfully assume the guise of uncommitted observers so carefully nurtured by mediators and so essential to their success.[25]

Consequences

David Shaw, writing in the *Hartford Courant* on May 27, 1984, noted, "The agreement is not a solution. It's the beginning of a new path of dealing with the same issues. It's going to require a great deal of cooperation. The issues have not gone away."

CARC v. *Thorne* Consent Decree Implementation Plan

Commissioner Thorne, Robert MacNamara, and the other defendants had responsibility for devising and implementing the remedial plan. The department had submitted two drafts of the implementation plan to the monitors by late summer 1984. However, the monitors felt it "fell short in the significant

[25]"Monitors: A New Equitable Remedy," *Yale Law Journal* 103 (1960).

areas of community placement and placement procedures, resource development, case management and quality assurance, staff training, and client safeguards in the areas of abuse and neglect, psychotropic medication, and restraints. As a result, the monitors "proposed the creation of five working groups—including representatives of the DMR central office, Mansfield Training School, the department's Regional Centers, other state agencies (the Departments of Income Maintenance and Health Services, the Office of Policy and Management, and the Attorney General), private community providers, long-term care facilities, plaintiff parent organizations (the CARC and MPA), DMR employees, and the Monitors—which would meet over a brief but concentrated period of time and agree on improvements to the plan."[26] The final plan was submitted to the court on April 25, 1985.

The *CARC* v. *Thorne* Consent Decree Implementation Plan, entitled "Hello, My Name Is Jenny," represented a collaborative effort to embody the spirit of the consent decree. In the Monitors Annual Report for May 1984–June 1985, the court monitors stated, "The Monitors cannot say enough about the seriousness and cooperative spirit with which all concerned participated in this worthwhile endeavor, which marked the first time many persons and interest groups affected by the Department's policies had had an opportunity to influence them."[27] It begins with the following introduction:

Hello, my name is Jenny, but I am many people for I am a CARC v. Thorne class member. For a long time, I have not responded much or well to the world around me. I lived at Mansfield; I live now in a nursing home.

But things are changing. A lot of people have been to see me, to wheel me around in my chair, to talk to me, to put objects in front of me and ask me to do things. Well, I surprised them all. I was not upset when new people arrived; I listened and I could do what they asked. I even understood in both French and English.

I'm not a young person, but I can do more than I've done so far. I have some strengths, some likes and dislikes. I might like a house with a few new friends in a neighborhood where people come and go . . . to have a picture of my father in my bedroom and some things of mine nearby . . . to visit my own doctor in his office . . . to go out to learn or work and come back to my home like other people do.

My name is Jenny, and though my name is not on every page, I'm there. So are David, Barry, Lisa, Allen, Rose. . . .[28]

[26]"Annual Report: Mansfield Class Panel of Monitors," May 1984–June 1985.
[27]Ibid.
[28]"Hello, My Name Is Jenny: CARC v. Thorne Consent Decree Implementation Plan," August 1985.

The comprehensive plan articulated four goals:

Goal I: Good practice and safeguards: Assure that services available to class members are coordinated and are available as prescribed, that class members have active representation in decision-making about their programs, are protected from abuse and harm, and have access to formal mechanisms to resolve disputes regarding service planning or provision.

Goal II: Comprehensive programs: With other state agencies, private providers, public and private community organizations, local municipalities and the federal government, continue to increase the availability of community placements for CARC v. Thorne class members. Assure that all class members, regardless of the severity of their handicap, have access to programs which promote independence and normalized life experiences, emphasize the use of generic services, and are integrated and comprehensive.

Goal III: Resource development and quality assurance: Develop mechanisms to ensure a maximum return on state funding for programs for CARC v. Thorne class members, including federal reimbursement, client access to existing community services, and effective quality assurance system, and an automated data system for tracking client placement and progress as well as staff utilization and performance.

Goal IV: Mansfield Training School: Continue efforts to enhance the quality of care and habilitation at Mansfield Training School, develop a plan for utilizing the facility as class members move to alternate placements.[29]

Specific, measurable objectives, necessary resources, and timetables were listed with each goal. See exhibit 4 for table of contents, which lists specific objectives.

Community Placement of Individual Plaintiffs

Although the consent decree mandated community placement of all individually named plaintiffs by June 1984, as of June 1985, only seven of the original twelve named plaintiffs had been placed in suitable community residences. Three of the plaintiffs remained in MTS, two in the New Haven Regional Center, two in a twenty-bed DMR facility, and one in a nursing home. One individual plaintiff remains at MTS as of this writing.

During the eighteen months from July 1, 1985, through December 31, 1986, a total of 45 class members requiring long-term care moved to community residences. A small number of class members entered long-term care facilities for convalescent or medical care. The number of class members in

[29]Ibid.

long-term care facilities decreased from 237 on July 1, 1985, to 182 on December 31, 1986. While long-term placements for 160 class members were expected in the period 1985–86 and 1986–87, only 45 long-term class members were placed in community settings by December 31, 1986. It is expected that an additional 60–76 persons will be placed by June 30, 1987.[30] Under the current system, the regions, not Mansfield Training School, are responsible for community placement.

Supported Employment

The supported employment program was established in February 1985 and was attributed to the department's original draft implementation plan of May 9, 1984, and elaborated in the final implementation plan. The monitors' 1984–85 annual report explains:

Both competitive and supported employment is usually compensated at the minimum wage and is supplemented by training, supervision, transportation, behavior management and any other service or activity needed to sustain the client in his or her position. The supported employment approach is much more integrated with the surrounding community and much more oriented toward productive work experience than traditional day services such as sheltered workshops and adult activity programs.[31]

Policies

As a consequence of the consent decree, thirteen policies regarding clients rights and treatment were developed and implemented in March 1986. The policies pertain to clients' rights, abuse and neglect, client programs, behavior modification medications, program review committee, human rights committees, programmatic administrative review, case management, eligibility for DMR services, program placements, overall plan of services, discharge, and advocates.

Annual Report: Manfield Class Panel of Monitors, May 1984–June 1985

The annual report developed by the Mansfield Class Panel of Monitors for the year May 1984–June 1985 and submitted to the Honorable F. Owen Eagan, U.S. magistrate, reported the following:

[30]"Status Report and Workplan: *CARC* v. *Thorne*, Long-Term Care Class Members," Connecticut Department of Mental Retardation, January 1987.
[31]"Annual Report, Mansfield Class Panel of Monitors," May 1984–June 1985.

In the year since the Mansfield Class Panel of Monitors was appointed in May 1984, the Monitors have seen vast changes in the operation and orientation of the Connecticut Department of Mental Retardation nursing homes and other such facilities. At this writing, the plan has been submitted to the Court and negotiations are proceeding on a relatively small number of unresolved issues. The department has developed and begun to carry out a comprehensive plan for implementation of the CARC v. Thorne Consent Decree that reflects an entirely new approach to such matters as community planning and placement, work-oriented day programs, and extension of community habilitative services to residents of MTS.

Other major developments during the year have included community placement of some (but far from all) the named individual plaintiffs, partial resolution of programming and safety issues in two Mansfield Training School buildings (Bennet Hall and Knight Hospital), completion of an audit of professional and direct care staffing at MTS, and development of new mechanisms for resolution of programmatic and placement disputes. All this has been accomplished in an atmosphere of lessening tension and increased cooperation, notwithstanding the fact that the Court has twice been asked to intervene in controversial situations."[32]

Reflections

The modified proposed consent decree has, in effect, mandated the state of Connecticut and MTS to set up an entirely new system of care. In its idealized form, this system of care would (1) emphasize community-based residential and habilitative services, (2) minimize the number of residents of MTS, and (3) move the system of care from a budget-based to a client-based system.

The broad positive consequences of the consent decree are notable. It resulted in a greater public awareness of the conditions, constraints, and opportunities of the mentally retarded in Connecticut. Through the negotiations during the six-year ordeal, the parties involved developed a greater, if not absolute, mutual shared understanding of the conditions of and opportunities for the mentally retarded population in the state. Most important, for many mentally retarded people, residential and habilitative opportunities that had been closed for years had finally been opened to them. Many adapted well to the changes. Others did not.

Through their experiences during the two and one-half years after the magistrate signed the modified proposed consent decree, the parties involved have gained a greater understanding of the difficult issues that can arise from such a decree. Some, but by far not all, of these issues are presented below.

[32]*Hartford Courant,* May 24, 1984.

The slow transition. Although the terms of the modified proposed consent decree regarding community placement were fairly consistent with the goals and recommendations enumerated in Project Challenge, the Department of Mental Retardation's 1973 long-term plan, progress has been slow. The large, complex bureaucracy of the Department of Mental Retardation, for so long embedded in an institutional model of care, now finds itself in a period of transition during which it must staff, monitor, and fund both an institutional and a community-based system of care. And since community-based systems are fairly new in the long history of service to those who are labeled mentally retarded, state employees at all levels find themselves learning about community services largely through hands-on experience.

One bureaucracy—two directions. In the years following the MTS consent decree, the U.S. Justice Department investigated Southbury Training School and, based on that investigation, filed a complaint which eventually resulted in another consent decree. Rather than emphasizing the development of community-based services, the Southbury consent decree emphasizes the improvement of standards of care at the institution and renovation of existing facilities. The problematic challenge before the state of Connecticut bureaucracy is to respond to two consent decrees: one which emphasizes community development and one which emphasizes institutional development. "It is," according to Mr. Lottman, "very hard for a bureaucracy to go in two directions at the same time."

The privileged class. There has been concern that a consent decree of this sort sets up a privileged class, one in which MTS clients are perceived as receiving attention and benefit at the expense of others, creating a dual system of services.

Mansfield Training School. There is concern that, as a result of the emphasis on community development, there will be less emphasis on the quality of life at Mansfield. Also, as a result of the halt on admissions, the remaining population is getting older, requiring changes in the types of services offered.

Community residences. Private providers, most of which are relatively new, nonprofit organizations, operate the community residences to which class members are placed. "Wages in Connecticut's private sector were 8–17% lower than for comparable occupations in selected other states and nationally. More dramatic was the finding that private sector wages lagged behind identical public sector positions by 56% in June of 1986, and that this differential increases to 64% by January 1987 . . . turnover in the private sector [is] 71% versus 25% for the public sector."[33]

A Syracuse study group found the following problems with respect to the

[33]"Compensation Study Executive Summary," November 1986.

community training homes: ambiguous definition and mission of community homes; confusion with the needs of children versus the needs of adults; discouragement of permanency and adoption for children; unclear authority of DMR central office vis-à-vis regions regarding community training home program; "funding of community training homes is cumbersome, complicated, and inequitable"; "inadequate supports to insure successful placements"; inadequate training for regional staff and staff of community training homes; inadequate monitoring; inadequate regional accountability; and underdevelopment of the community training home program.[34]

The labor force. A major organizational consequence has been the impact of the consent decree on the labor force. Pat Staszko-Kozik, director of MTS, describes the effect of the consent decree on the direct-care employees as a type of "schizophrenia." On the one hand, direct-care staff view their role as trying to improve the quality of care and services. On the other hand, they are aware that many of the institutionalized services they provide have been publically devalued in an institution that is seen as closing. On a practical level, they fear for their jobs because as MTS phases down in clients, they phase down in staff. At a time when quality direct-care staff is needed, MTS is not an attractive place from the recruitment standpoint. Both the Department of Mental Retardation and District 1199 have addressed the concerns of direct-care staff. The employees have received a generous contract. District 1199's contract includes deinstutionalization provisions, and the state has made a commitment not to lay off employees.

Changing roles. A great deal of time has been spent reinventing legitimate roles for groups in a system that has outgrown the traditional role played by these groups. The board of trustees, required by law and appointed by the governor, have lost both decision-making authority and power as a result of the consent decree. The decisions of who/how/what have been taken out of their hands, and in reality, it seems to them as though the court monitors are the board of trustees.

The Mansfield Foundation, primarily a fund-raising organization, floundered, uncertain of its role and usefulness, for some time after the signing of the consent decree. How should such a group raise funds for improvements on a place that is not going to be there long-term? After a period of questioning its role, the foundation began to consider alternatives, among them the purchasing of adaptive equipment and computerized communication devices, as well as establishing a scholarship at the University of Connecticut.

---

[34]"An Evaluation of Connecticut's Community Training Home Program," by Steven Taylor, Zana Lutfiyya, Julie Racino, Pam Walker, and James Knoll (Syracuse University, June 1986).

MPA concerns. While CARC parents and advocates anxiously await community placement for class members, many Mansfield parents are frightened of what community placement may mean for their children. Said Pat Staszko-Kozik, "They hang on to the hope that their children will be one of the 120 expected to remain at Mansfield."

The receiving communities. Zoning battles are not unknown.

Two and one-half years after the signing of the modified proposed consent decree, several questions remain, among them: Why has the consent decree not been as successful as hoped by the CARC, as mandated by the decree itself, and as planned for in the implementation plan? How does a state manage the transition from an institutional to a community model, balancing clinical needs, speed, available knowledge and experience, and budgetary constraints? What are the ethical dilemmas that arise from a class action suit? And what will happen when the court-appointed monitors leave, possibly at the end of 1987?

Exhibit One: Parties in the Case during Initial Years of Litigation

Plaintiffs

Connecticut Association for Retarded Citizens. "A non-profit organization created in 1951 and existing under the laws of the state of Connecticut, with offices at 15 High Street, Hartford, Connecticut, 27 member chapters and a membership of 6,000 families statewide. The purpose of the Association is to promote the general welfare of mentally retarded persons in the State of Connecticut." Members include parents, other relatives, guardians, and friends of persons at Mansfield and at risk of being placed at Mansfield.

William Brilla, Allan Ricardi, David Meli, Joseph Rittlinger, Marion Rogers, Gary Rotonto, Stephen Ogren, Tina Sandahl, Philip Teitelman, Kristina Arnold, Stuwart Clair, and Lisa French. Named plaintiffs in the claim.

David Shaw. Attorney for the individual plaintiffs. He eventually ended up representing the Mansfield Parents Association as well.

Frank J. Laski. Attorney for the CARC.

Defendants

Gareth Thorne. "Commissioner of the Department of Mental Retardation for the State of Connecticut. He is responsible for the planning and development of a complete, comprehensive and integrated state-wide program for the mentally retarded; for the implementation of said program; and for the coordination of the efforts of the Department of Mental Retardation with other state departments and agencies, municipal governments, and private agencies concerned with and providing services for the mentally retarded. He is responsible for the administration and operation of the state training schools, regional centers, and all state-operated community and residential facilities established for the diagnosis, care, and training of the retarded. He is responsible for the development of criteria as to the eligibility of any retarded person for residential care in any public or state-supported private institution and, after considering the recommendation of a properly designated diagnostic agency, may assign such person to a public or state-supported private institution. He may transfer such person from one institution to another when necessary and desirable for his welfare."

Roger MacNamara. "Superintendent of Mansfield Training School, responsible for the operation and administration of the Training School and for the custody and control of all persons admitted to the Training School. He is responsible for authorizing transfers into and out of the Training School, from or to another state facility for the mentally retarded, or a state hospital for the mentally ill."

Francis Maloney. "Commissioner of the Department of Children and Youth Services for the State of Connecticut. The Department is required by statute to develop and maintain a program of day treatment centers for emotionally disturbed, mentally ill and autistic children and youth and to operate a central residential facility for the care, training, treatment, and rehabilitation of autistic children and youth, and for children and youth who exhibit both emotional and mental disturbance and retarded intellectual functioning."

Mr. Marcus. Successor to office of Mr. Maloney and substituted as defendant.

Edward Maher. "Commissioner of the Department of Social Services for the State of Connecticut. . . . [He is] responsible for the enforcement of provisions of Title XIX and the Social Security Act in this state. The Act requires independent view of the need of persons placed in skilled nursing facilities for the level of medical care providing by such facilities prior to admission to a skilled nursing facility and that periodic inspections be made in all skilled nursing facilities. . . . [He] is also responsible for enforcement of similar provisions of the social security act written to ensure that inappropriate placements in intermediate care facilities are not made and that independent professional reviews are conducted to identify persons inappropriately placed in such facilities."

Mr. Heintz. Successor in office to Mr. Maher and substituted as defendant in case.

Douglas Lloyd. "Commissioner of the Department of Health for the State of Connecticut. The Department issues licenses for the operation and maintenance of all hospitals, homes for the aged, nursing homes, and rest homes in the state. Licenses may be issued only upon inspection and investigation, and upon the finding by the Department that the applicant and facilities meet requirements established by the Department to promote safe, humane, and adequate care."

Amicus Curiae

U.S. Justice Department. Joined procedures in December 1979 as litigating amicus curiae.

Connecticut Conference of Municipalities and the National Association for Retarded Citizens.

Assistant Attorney David Whinston. Represented the U.S. Justice Department in the suit.

Other Parties

Mansfield Parents Association. Organization representing approximately 450 families with children or siblings at MTS. Its exclusive focus is the welfare of Mansfield residents.

New England Health Care Employees Union District 1199 of the National Union of Hospital and Health Care employees, AFL-CIO. Union representing approximately 1,000 direct-care employees at MTS, approximately 2,000 employees in 23 nursing homes, and some employees of community programs (JFF 17).

Joel I. Klein. Counsel for Intervenors, MPA, et al.

Court Monitors

Four-member panel. Dr. Susan Brody Hasazi (Vermont), chairperson; Mr. Urbano (Ben) Censoni (Michigan), vice chairperson; Dr. Ronald Melzer (Vermont); Mr. Eddie Moore (New Jersey).

Staff members. Mr. Michael Lottman, executive director; Ms. Barbara Jean Roskos.

Judge

Hon. F. Owen Eagan. Presiding U.S. magistrate.

Source: "Original Complaint."

Exhibit Two: Plaintiff's Original Claims

Count I: Equal Protection Claim

By forcing plaintiffs to submit to segregation in order to receive ineffective public services, while the rest of the citizenry receives a wide range of effective services in the community, the defendants have denied plaintiffs the equal protection of the laws, secured to them by the Equal Protection Clause of the Fourteenth Amendment.

Count II: Rehabilitation Act Claims

Section 504 of the Rehabilitation Act of 1973, 29 U.S.C. section 794, provides: "no otherwise qualified handicapped individual in the United States . . . shall, solely by reason of his handicap, be excluded from participation in, be denied the benefits of, or be subjected to discrimination under any program or activity receiving federal financial assistance." By failing to provide retarded persons effective services delivered in the least separate, most integrated, least restrictive environment, defendants have violated plaintiffs' rights secured by 29 U.S.C. section 794.

Count III: Constitutional Claims

The acts and omissions of the defendants deny plaintiffs their constitutional rights:

(a) to the habilitation necessary to enable plaintiffs to speak, read, communicate, associate and assemble with others of their choice and otherwise exercise their rights under the First Amendment;

(b) to privacy, liberty, dignity, and family integrity under the First, Fourth, Fifth, Ninth, and Fourteenth Amendments;

(c) to freedom from invidious discrimination on grounds of wealth under the Equal Protection Clause of the Fourteenth Amendment;

(d) to an individualized habilitation plan and program under the Due Process and Equal Protection Clauses of the Fourteenth Amendment;

(e) to the opportunity to be heard on the appropriateness of the plan, program, and environment of treatment and in periodic review thereof, under the Due Process Clause of the Fourteenth Amendment;

(f) to a friend-advocate to assist each plaintiff to live safely in freedom, under the First Amendment, and the Due Process and Equal Protection Clauses of the Fourteenth Amendment;

(g) lastly, to protection from harm and to individualized treatment and habilitation in the least restrictive environment under the Due Process Clause of the Fourteenth Amendment and under the Eighth Amendment.

Count IV: Social Security Act Claim

Defendants, recipients of federal funds, are in violation of 42 U.S.C. section 1396a by failing to evaluate the appropriateness of placement of plaintiffs in Title XIX facilities and the feasibility of meeting their needs through alternative institutional or noninstitutional care.

Count V: Developmental Disabilities Act Claim

Defendants are in violation of 42 U.S.C. section 6010 by failing to develop and periodically review habilitation plans and programs for plaintiffs and to provide them effective services in the least separate, most integrated, least restrictive environment.

Source: "Original Complaint," pp. 48–50.

Exhibit Three: Relief Requested by Plaintiffs

WHEREFORE, plaintiffs respectfully request that this Court:

1. Permanently enjoin defendants to provide each plaintiff and member of the plaintiff class effective services in the least separate, most integrated, least restrictive community setting appropriate to their needs.

2. Preliminarily and permanently enjoin defendants from admitting persons to Mansfield or from transferring present residents from Mansfield unless such transfer is to the least separate, most integrated, least restrictive community setting appropriate to their needs, ancillary and necessary services provided.

3. Preliminarily and permanently enjoin defendants to make available in advance of that time and with dispatch the necessary alternative residential facilities and services in the community.

4. Preliminarily and permanently enjoin defendants to develop written individualized habilitation and exit plans for each plaintiff and member of the plaintiffs' class and to provide an individualized habilitation program for each.

5. Preliminarily and permanently enjoin defendants to make available a friend-advocate to each plaintiff and member of the plaintiffs' class to assist each in securing the substantive and procedural protections aforesaid.

6. Declare unconstitutional, and unlawful under . . . the Rehabilitation Act of 1973 the failure of defendants to provide plaintiffs and members of the class with effective services delivered in the least separate, most integrated, least restrictive community setting, and preliminarily and permanently enjoin them to provide such services.

7. Preliminarily and permanently enjoin defendants from failing to perform their duties under other federal statutes (42 U.S.C. section 6010 and 42 U.S.C. section 1396a).

8. Preliminarily and permanently enjoin defendants to submit to plaintiffs and to the Court for its approval a plan for implementation of the aforesaid.

9. Enter a final judgment certifying the class of individual plaintiffs represent to include all persons who are now at Mansfield or who may be transferred there in the future; retarded persons residing at home who, because effective community services to assist their families are unavailable, are in jeopardy of being sent to Mansfield; and persons who have been transferred to skilled nursing facilities, intermediate care facilities, homes for the aged, and similar facilities, yet remain Mansfield's responsibility, and who, because of defendants' failure to provide alternatives in the community, may be forced to return to Mansfield.

10. Award plaintiffs costs and attorneys' fees.

11. Award plaintiffs and members of plaintiffs class such other relief as is necessary to effectuate their rights to effective services in an integrated community setting.

Source: "Original Claim, pp. 51–53.

Exhibit Four: *CARC* v. *Thorne* Consent Decree Implementation Plan, Goals and Objectives

Goal I: Good Practice and Safeguards

Assure that services available to class members are coordinated and are available as prescribed, that class members have active representation in decision-making about their programs, are protected from abuse and harm, and have access to formal mechanisms to resolve disputes regarding service planning or provision.

Objectives:

1. Parental involvement
2. Advocates
3. Case management
4. Interdisciplinary team process
5. Dispute resolution
6. Safeguards: Abuse
7. Safeguards: Psychotropic medication and restraint
8. Staff training

Goal II: Comprehensive Programs

With other state agencies, private providers, public and private community organizations, local municipalities and the federal government, continue to increase the availability of community placements for *CARC* v. *Thorne* class members. Assure that all class members, regardless of the severity of their handicap, have access to programs which promote independence and normalized life experiences, emphasize the use of generic services, and are integrated and comprehensive.

Objectives:

9. Placement process
10. Community placements
11. Long-term care
12. Day programs
13. Program support staff

Goal III: Resource Development and Quality Assurance

Develop mechanisms to ensure a maximum return on state funding for programs for *CARC* v. *Thorne* class members, including federal reimbursement, client access to existing community services, an effective quality assurance system, and an automated data system for tracking client placement and progress as well as staff utilization and performance.

Objectives:

14. Enhancing regional resources

15. Maximizing resources

16. Automated data system

17. Quality assurance

Goal IV: Mansfield Training School

Continue efforts to enhance the quality of care and habilitation at Mansfield Training School, develop a plan for utilizing the facility as class members move to alternate placements.

Objectives:

18. Projections for client and bed reductions

19. Physical plant

20. Advocacy

21. Training

22. Day programs

23. Bennet Hall

24. Wyatt-Stickney compliance

Source: "*CARC* v. *Thorne* Consent Decree Implementation Plan," August 1984.

Selected Bibliography

Books

Bass, Jack. *Unlikely Heroes*. New York: Simon and Schuster, 1981.

Bullock, Charles S. III, and Charles M. Lamb, eds. *Implementation of Civil Rights Policy*. Monterey, Calif.: Brooks/Cole, 1984.

Cooper, Phillip J. *Hard Judicial Choices: Federal District Court Judges and State and Local Officials*. New York and Oxford: Oxford University Press, 1988.

———. *Public Law and Public Administration*. 2d ed. Englewood Cliffs, N.J.: Prentice-Hall, 1988.

Fisher, Louis. *Constitutional Dialogues: Interpretation as Political Process*. Princeton: Princeton University Press, 1988.

Hanis, M. Kay, and Dudley P. Spriller, Jr. *After Decision: Implementation of Judicial Decrees in Correctional Settings*. Washington, D.C.: National Institute of Law Enforcement and Criminal Justice, 1977.

Hochschild, Jennifer. *The New American Dilemma*. New Haven: Yale University Press, 1984.

Horowitz, Donald L. *The Courts and Social Policy*. Washington, D.C.: The Brookings Institution, 1977.

Katzmann, Robert A., ed. *Judges and Legislators: Toward Institutional Comity*. Washington, D.C.: The Brookings Institution, 1988.

Kelman, Steven. *Making Public Policy: A Hopeful View of American Government*. New York: Basic Books, 1987.

Murphy, Walter F. *Congress and the Court: A Case Study in the American Political Process*. Chicago: University of Chicago Press, 1962.

Peltason, Jack W. *Fifty-eight Lonely Men: Southern Judges and School Desegregation*. Urbana: University of Illinois Press, 1971.

Scheingold, Stuart. *The Politics of Rights: Lawyers, Public Policy, and Political Change*. New Haven: Yale University Press, 1974.

Shapiro, Martin M. *Who Guards the Guardians: Judicial Control of Administration*. Athens: University of Georgia Press, 1988.

Yarbrough, Tinsley. *Judge Frank M. Johnson and Human Rights in Alabama*. University: University of Alabama Press, 1981.

Articles

Bazelon, David L. "Implementing the Rights to Treatment." 36 *University of Chicago Law Review* 742 (1969).

Bickel, Alexander, and Harry Wellington. "Legislative Purpose and the Judicial Process: The Lincoln Mills Case." 71 *Harvard Law Review* (November 1957).

Bunbaum, Morton. "The Right to Treatment." 46 *American Bar Association Journal* 499 (1960).

Cavanagh, Ralph, and Austin Sarat. "Thinking About Courts: Toward and Beyond a Jurisprudence of Judicial Competence." 14 *Law and Society Review* 371 (1980).

Chayes, Abram. "The Role of the Judge in Public Law Litigation." 89 *Harvard Law Review* 1281 (1979).

Coffin, Frank M. "*The Federalist* Number 86: On Relations Between the Judiciary and Congress." 4 *Brookings Review* (Winter–Spring 1986).

Cranton, Roger C. "Judicial Policy Making and Administration," 31 *Public Administration Review* 551 (1976).

Dienes, C. Thomas. "Judges, Legislators, and Social Change." 13 *American Behavioral Scientist* (March–April 1970).

Diver, Colin. "The Judge as Powerbroker: Superintending Change in Political Institutions." 65 *Virginia Law Review* 43 (1979).

———. "Statutory Interpretation in the Administrative State." 133 *University of Pennsylvania Law Review* 3 (1985).

Easterbrook, Frank H. "The Supreme Court 1983 Term—Foreword: The Court and the Economic System." 98 *Harvard Law Review* 4 (1984).

Fuller, Lon. "The Forms and Limits of Adjudication." 92 *Harvard Law Review* 353 (1978).

Gerwin, Leslie E. "The Deference Dilemma: Judicial Responses to the Great Legislative Power Giveaway." 14 *Hastings Constitutional Law Quarterly* 289 (1987).

Gilmour, Robert S. "Agency Administration by Judiciary." 6 *Southern Review of Public Administration* 26 (1982).

Glazer, Nathan. "Should Courts Administer Social Services." 50 *Public Interest* 64 (1978).

Henschen, Beth. "Statutory Interpretations of the Supreme Court: Congressional Response." 11 *American Politics Quarterly* (January 1983): pp. 441–457.

Johnson, Frank M. "The Constitution and the Federal District Judge." 54 *Texas Law Review* 903 (1976).

Katzmann, Robert A. "Approaching the Bench: Judicial Confirmation in Perspective." 6 *Brookings Review* (Spring 1988): 42–46.

Macey, Jonathan. "Promoting Public-Regarding Legislation through Statutory Interpretation: An Interest Group Model." 86 *Columbia Law Review* (1986).

Mashaw, Jerry L. "Prodelegation: Why Administrators Should Make Political Decisions." 1 *Journal of Law, Economics, and Organization* 81 (1985).

Melnick, R. Shep, "The Politics of Partnership." 45 *Public Administration Review* (November 1985): 653–60.

"The Mentally Ill and the Right to Treatment." 36 *University of Chicago Law Review* 742 (1969).

Nathan, Vincent M. "The Use of Masters in Institutional Reform Litigation." 10 *Toledo Law Review* 419 (1979).

"Observations on the Right to Treatment." 57 *Georgetown Law Journal* 673 (1969).

Resnick, Judith. "Managerial Judges," 96 *Harvard Law Review* 374 (1982).

Starr, Kenneth. "Judicial Review of Administrative Action in a Conservative Era." 39 *Administrative Law Review* 353 (1987).

Stumpf, Harry. "Congressional Response to Supreme Court Rulings: The Interaction of Law and Politics." 14 *Journal of Public Law* 377 (1965).

Sunstein, Cass. "Legal Interference with Private Preferences." 53 *University of Chicago Law Review* 1129 (1986).

Wasby, Stephen L. "Arrogation of Power or Accountability: Judicial Imperialism Revisited." 65 *Judicature* 208 (1981).

"The Wyatt Case: Implementation of a Judicial Decree Ordering Institutional Change," 84 *Yale Law Journal* 1338 (1975).

Wood, Robert, "Professionals at Bay: Managing Boston's Public Schools." 1 *Journal of Policy Analysis and Management* 4 (1982): 454–68.

*The Organizational
Consequences of
Remedial Law: A
Working Conference*

Participants

Alan A. Altshuler, a political scientist, is Ruth and Frank Stanton Professor of
   Urban Policy and Planning and director for the Taubman Center for State
   and Local Government, John F. Kennedy School of Government, Harvard
   University. He has also taught at MIT, Swarthmore College, and Cornell
   University, and from 1969 to 1975 he held a series of positions in Mas-
   sachusetts state government. His books include *55: A Decade of Experience;
   The Urban Transportation System: Politics and Policy Innovation; Current
   Issues in Transportation Policy:* and *The Politics of the Federal Bureaucracy.*

James P. Breeden is dean of the William Jewett Tucker Foundation, Dartmouth
   College. Previously he was executive director of the Center for Law and
   Education, Inc.; senior officer, Office of Planning and Policy, Boston Public
   Schools; executive director of Citywide Coordinating Council, Boston. Dean
   Breeden was also executive director of the Commission on Church and Race,
   Massachusetts Council of Churches; a canon and adviser on civil rights,
   Cathedral Church of St. Paul, Diocese of Massachusetts; and curate at St.
   James' Episcopal Church, Roxbury, Massachusetts.

Alvin J. Bronstein is the executive director of the National Prison Project of the
   American Civil Liberties Union Foundation. At various times since 1959 he
   has been a consultant and/or trial counsel to CORE, NAACP, NAACP Legal
   Defense Fund, SNCC, SCLC, Mississippi Freedom Democratic Party, Black

Panther Party, National Institute for Education in Law and Poverty, and consumer, welfare rights, civil rights, and community organizations throughout the country. His books include *Prisoners and the Courts: The American Experience* (contributing author); *The Prison Journal* (contributing author); *Our Endangered Rights* (contributing author); *The Rights of Prisoners* (with Rudovsky and Koren); and *Representing Prisoners*.

Phillip J. Cooper is chair of the Department of Political Science at the State University of New York at Albany. He has also taught at the University of Utah, Mississippi State University, and Georgia State University. His books include *Hard Judicial Choices: Federal District Judges and State and Local Officials; Public Law and Public Administration; Of Power and Right: Justice William O. Douglas and Hugo Black* (with Howard Ball).

Margaret Dignoti is executive director of the Connecticut Association of Retarded Citizens.

John A. Finger, Jr., is a professor of education, with a joint appointment in the Psychology Department and the Department of Counseling and Educational Psychology, Rhode Island College. He is an associate at the Center for Evaluation and Research of Rhode Island College. His professional interests are school desegregation, educational psychology, and data processing for statistical analysis, testing, and evaluation. Significant past activities include consultant to Massachusetts State Board of Education for School Desegregation; court-appointed consultant, Federal District Court, master for *Brinkman* vs. *Gilligan,* Dayton, Ohio; court-appointed consultant, Federal District Court, *Milliken* vs. *Bradley,* Detroit, Michigan; court-appointed consultant, Federal District Court, Washington Parish, Louisiana; court-appointed consultant, Federal District Court, *Keyes* vs. *School District No. One,* Denver, Colorado; court-appointed consultant, Federal District Court, *Swann* vs. *Board of Education, Charlotte-Mechlenburg County.*

Paul G. Garrity is a partner at McGrath, Kane & Garrity; in general practice; and a specialist in civil litigation and business representation. He is an instructor of civil trial practice at Boston College Law School and Northeastern University Law School; a team leader, Trial Advocacy Institute, Massachusetts Continuing Legal Education; member of the board of directors and instructor of trial and civil motion practice programs for Advocacy Training Institute, Boston. From 1976 to 1984 he was justice of the Massachusetts Superior Court, the circuit trial court of general jurisdiction for the Commonwealth of Massachusetts. He has presided at major, mostly civil jury, trials—approximately fifty each year.

W. Arthur Garrity, Jr., a United States district judge since July 7, 1966 (Boston, Massachusetts). He is a graduate of Holy Cross and the Harvard Law School. He has been a panelist at Joint Sentencing Institute of First and

Second Circuits; a panelist on criminal law at Circuit Conference of Third Circuit; Circuit Council of First Judicial Circuit, member 1983–85; Judicial Conference of the United States, member of standing committee on administration of the criminal law, 1969–75, and member of conference 1982–85.

Willis D. Hawley is dean of the George Peabody College, Vanderbilt University, and professor of education and political science. Previously he was director, Center for Education and Human Development Policy, and director, Program in Educational Equity at Vanderbilt Institute of Public Policy Studies; director, Center for Educational Policy, Duke University; study director, Education Study, President's Reorganization Project, U.S. Office of Management and Budget. His books include *The Politics of Federal Government Reorganization; Achieving Quality Integrated Education; Good Schools: A Synthesis of Research on How Schools Influence Student Achievement: The Consequences of School Desegregation; Strategies for Effective Desegregation: Lessons from Research; Effective School Desegregation: Equity, Quality, and Feasibility.*

Donald L. Horowitz is professor of law, public policy studies and political science at Duke University, receiving his LL.M. and Ph.D. from Harvard University. He was an attorney with the Department of Justice, Civil Division, Appellate Section, Washington, D.C.; a fellow, Council on Foreign Relations and Woodrow Wilson International Center for Scholars, a research associate, the Brookings Institution; a senior fellow, Research Institute on Immigration and Ethnic Studies, the Smithsonian Institution. His books include *Ethnic Groups in Conflict; Coup Theories and Officers' Motives: Sri Lanka in Comparative Perspective; The Jurocracy: Government Lawyers, Agency Programs, and Judicial Decisions;* and *The Courts and Social Policy.*

Marshall Kaplan is dean and professor, Graduate School of Public Affairs, University of Colorado. He was deputy assistant secretary, Department of Housing and Urban Development, and deputy director of the Ford Foundation funded Community Development Project at the University of California. The project evaluated the New Town Movement in the nation and produced a book written by Dean Kaplan and Edward Eichler called *The Community Builders.* Kaplan's other books include *Federal Decision Making and Impact in Urban Areas: A Study of Oakland; Urban Growth and Land Development: The Land Conversion Process; Urban Planning in the 1960s, a Design for Irrelevancy; The Politics of Neglect: From Model Cities to Revenue Sharing.*

Robert A. Katzmann is a senior fellow, research associate, guest scholar at the Brookings Institution. He is also president of the Governance Institute to promote research and discussion on problems of governance with emphasis on law institutions and policymaking, and he is special assistant to the director of the Federal Judicial Center. His Ph.D. is from Harvard University. His publications include *Institutional Disability: The Saga of Transportation Policy for the Disabled; Regulatory Bureaucracy: The Federal Trade Commission and Antitrust Policy; In Proud and Silent Isolation: On Relations between the Judiciary and Congress;* and forthcoming, *Proceedings of the Colloquium on Judicial-Congressional Relations.*

Herbert Kaufman received his Ph.D. from Columbia University and has taught at Yale and at Boston College, where he was the Thomas P. O'Neill, Jr., Professor of American Politics. He has been a senior fellow and guest scholar at the Brookings Institution, a visiting scholar at the Russel Sage Foundation, and a staff member, task force member, and consultant at various times to federal, state, and local agencies. Recent books of his include *Time, Chance, and Organizations: Natural Selections in a Perilous Environment; The Administrative Behavior of Federal Bureau Chiefs; Red Tape: Its Origins, Uses, and Abuses;* and *Are Governments Immortal?*

Brian R. Lensink is commissioner, State of Connecticut, Department of Mental Retardation. Previously he was assistant deputy director, Department of Economic Security, Office of Intergovernmental Operation, Arizona; executive director, Human Services Agency, Nebraska; executive director, Eastern Nebraska Community Office of Retardation; program director, Greater Omaha Association for Retarded Children; trainer, teacher, and evaluator at Christ Child Services, Occupational Training Center, Minnesota. His books include *Shaping the Future: Community-Based Residential Services and Facilities for Mentally Retarded People; Changing Patterns in Residential Services for the Mentally Retarded; New Neighbors: The Retarded Citizen in Quest of a Home.*

R. Shep Melnick is associate professor of politics at Brandeis University. His Ph.D. dissertation from Harvard is entitled "Into the Regulatory Thicket: The Impact of Court Decision on Federal Regulation of Air Pollution." He is currently working on "Judicial Activism and the New Congress," an examination of the interaction between Congress and the courts in four policy areas: AFDC, Food Stamps, education of the handicapped, and Title I of ESEA.

Ronald Melzer is director of Mental Retardation, Vermont Department of Mental Health. Previously he was chief, Liaison Services, Multi-state Information System, Rockland State Hospital Research Center, New York. His Ph.D. is in psychology from the University of Vermont and he has taught there and at Vassar College. He is on the board of directors of the National Association of State Mental Retardation Program Directors, and he served as a member of the Mansfield Class Panel of Monitors for *CARC* vs. *Thorne Consent Decree.*

John J. Moran is the director of the Rhode Island State Department of Corrections. He received his undergraduate degree in sociology and his master of science degree in social work from Boston College. He also has been director, Arizona State Department of Corrections; director, Division of Adult Corrections, State of Delaware; director, Division of Juvenile Corrections, State of Delaware; superintendent, Vermont Youth Center, State of Vermont; associate warden, Vermont State Prison; executive director, United Prison Association, Massachusetts; superintendent, Institute for Juvenile Guidance, Massachusetts.

Russell D. Murphy has been professor of government at Wesleyan since 1966. He was a member of the editorial board for *American Political Science Review* and is a member of the Council of the Connecticut Chapter of the American Society for Public Administration. He has served as director and president of the Middlesex County Legal Assistance Association, as chair of the Task Force on Staffing for the Middletown Board of Education, and as a member of the State Legislative Election Committee Study Group on Election Law. Among his publications are "Whither the Mayors: A Note on Mayoral Careers," *Journal of Politics* (February 1980); "The Mayoralty and the New Democracy: The Evolution of an Ideology and an Institution," *Urban Affairs Quarterly* (Sept. 1986); and *Political Entrepreneurs and Urban Poverty.*

James P. Scamman was superintendent of the Denver Public Schools, 1985: Before that he was superintendent of the South Bend Community School Corporation in Indiana and superintendent of the Stevens Point Area Public Schools in Wisconsin; he was also administrator of Planning and Research for the Kenosha, Wisconsin, schools. His Ph.D., from Iowa State University, is in educational administration. He has written "Assignment and Teacher Preparation," which appeared in the *Journal of Educational Research;* "Decade Ahead: Critical Issues Facing Schools," President's Committee for a National Agenda for the Eighties; and "Schools for the 21st Century," presented for Education Week, Chautauqua, New York.

David C. Shaw is associated with the Hartford law firm of Trowbridge, Ide, Courtney & Mansfield, P.C., specializing in litigation on behalf of disabled citizens and in personal injury litigation. Previously he practiced law as a staff attorney for the Legal Aid Society of Hartford County, Inc., where he also specialized in litigation on behalf of disabled citizens. His degree is from the University of Connecticut School of Law, and he is a graduate of the National Institute for Trial Advocacy, Boulder, Colorado. He was instrumental in obtaining consent decree in *CARC* vs. *Thorne.*

Lewis H. Spence is lecturer of public policy at the John F. Kennedy School of Government, Harvard University, and vice president of development management, The Beacon Companies, Boston. He was the court-appointed received of the Boston Housing Authority. He served both as chief executive officer of the BHA and assumed all policy formulating responsiblity previously carried out by the board. His publications include "the Strategic Role of Public Space," *Post-war Public Housing in Trouble;* "Reagan's Big Lie," *Boston Observer;* "Technology and the Poor," *Technology Review;* and "Opinion and Comment: Public Housing Disorder," *Journal of Housing.*

Robert B. Whittlesey has been executive director of the Boston Housing Partnership, Inc.—a consortium of business, communities, and government whose goal is to provide affordable housing in Boston's neighborhoods—since October 1983. Mr. Whittlesey was founding executive director of Greater Boston Community Development, Inc., a nonprofit organization that provides technical assistance to community-based sponsors of low- and moderate-income housing. From 1975 until 1980 he was the court-appointed master in the *Perez et al.* vs. *Boston Housing Authority* case.

Robert C. Wood is the Henry R. Luce Professor of Democratic Institutions and the Social Order at Wesleyan. He was superintendent of the Boston Public Schools, president of the University of Massachusetts, chairman of the Massachusetts Bay Transportation Authority, and secretary and undersecretary of the United States Department of Housing and Urban Development during the Johnson Administration. He has also taught at MIT, the University of Massachusetts, and Harvard. Presently, he is chair of the Governor's Coalition for Literacy in Connecticut, and he was chair of the Twentieth Century Fund Task Force on Federal Education Policy. His books include *The Necessary Majority: Middle America and the Urban Crisis; Politics and Government in the United States; 1400 Governments, the Political Economy of the New York Metropolitan Region; Suburbia: Its People and Their Politics;* and *Metropolis against Itself.*

Commentators

Barbara Craig, associate professor of government, Wesleyan University
Robert Gilmour, professor of political science, University of Connecticut
Elaine Johansen, associate professor of political science, University of Connecticut
Charles C. Lemert, professor of sociology, Wesleyan University
Mark Moore, Daniel and Florence Guggenheim Professor of Criminal Justice Policy and Management, John F. Kennedy School of Government, Harvard University
Marcy M. Murninghan, president, Lighthouse Investment Group, Boston, Mass.
Jonathan Sack, Esq., formerly law clerk for Federal Judge Arthur Garrity
Mort Tenzer, associate professor of political science, University of Connecticut